WITHDRAWN

NASH LIBRARY
Univ. of Science & Arts of
Okla. - P.O. Box 82345
Chickasha, OK 73018-0001

D1404361

Native America Collected

Native America Collected
The Culture of an Art World

Margaret Dubin

UNIVERSITY OF NEW MEXICO PRESS

ALBUQUERQUE

© 2001 by The University of New Mexico Press
All rights reserved.
First edition

Library of Congress Cataloging-in-Publication Data:

Dubin, Margaret D., 1967–
    Native America collected : the culture of an art world / Margaret Dubin.— 1st ed.
        p.   cm.
Includes bibliographical references and index.
    ISBN 0-8263-2174-7 (cloth : alk. paper)
    1. Indian art—Collectors and collecting—United States—History.
    2. Indian art—United States—Public opinion. 3. Indians in popular culture.
    4. Tourist trade and art—United States—History. 5. Art museums—United States—
    Administration. 6. Art criticism—United States. 7. Public opinion—United States. I. Title.
E98.A7 D77 2001
381´.457040397073—dc21   2001000828

An earlier version of Chapter 6 appeared in *Native American Art in the Twentieth Century,* edited by W. Jackson Rushing (Routledge, 1999).

E
98
.A7D77
2001

to my parents

Contents

Illustrations   *vii*

Introduction   *1*

1. Objects Desired: A History of Collecting   *11*

2. Commodities Controlled:
   Legislating the Trade of Native American Art   *27*

3. Collectors: Charity, Empathy, Matching the Sofa   *49*

4. Artists: Selling Paintings, Dispelling Stereotypes   *65*

5. Museums and the Politics of Cultural Authority   *83*

6. Sanctioned Scribes: How Critics, Curators,
   and Scholars Write the Native American Art World   *101*

7. Collecting/Being Collected:
   The Language of Cultural Difference   *125*

Epilogue: Reflections on Fieldwork   *147*

Notes   *153*

Works Cited   *169*

Index   *179*

illustrations

I.1.   Alfred Boyd and Roy Dune Walters   *2*

I.2.   American Indian Community House Gallery/Museum   *7*

1.1   "Big Chief Series" by Joanna O. Bigfeather (Cherokee)   *14*

2.1–   "Would I have been a member of the Nighthawk,
2.3.   Snake society or would I have been a half breed
       leading the whites to the full bloods . . ."
       by Hulleah Tsinhnahjinnie (Seminole/Creek/Navajo)   *33–35*

2.4.   "Talking Leaves" (pages 5 and 6) by Kay WalkingStick (Cherokee)   *37*

2.5.   "Mass Producing a Tradition" by Nora Naranjo-Morse (Santa Clara)   *46*

3.1.   The hands of JR   *54*

3.2.   East Coast collectors Joan and Steve Fine   *60*

3.3.   Bev Rabinowitz holds a dinosaur pot by Andrew Pacheco (Santo Domingo)   *62*

4.1.   "Inner Flight" by Dan V. Lomahaftewa (Hopi)   *69*

4.2.   "Frog Hat" by Preston Singletary (Tlingit)   *75*

4.3.   "Raven Steals the Sun" by Preston Singletary (Tlingit)   *76*

5.1.   "This Path We Travel," National Museum of the American Indian   *91*

5.2. Museum of the American Indian ca. 1925   *93*

6.1. "Rushing Water" by Emmi Whitehorse (Navajo)   *111*

6.2. "Talking Leaves" (pages 11 and 12) by Kay WalkingStick (Cherokee)   *113*

6.3. "Stone Poem #43" by Harry Fonseca (Maidu)   *116*

6.4. "Angry Coyote" by Rick Bartow (Yurok)   *118*

6.5. "Many Moons" (detail) by Doug Coffin (Potawatomi/Creek)   *120*

7.1. "The Artifact Piece" by James Luna (Luiseño)   *132*

7.2. Untitled painting by Gerald Nailor (Navajo)   *138*

7.3 "Anthropological Mistake" (detail) by Joanna O. Bigfeather (Cherokee)   *144*

THE SUMMER OF 1987 found me on the Navajo reservation in northeastern Arizona, living with a Navajo family and conducting fieldwork for my college thesis, an ethnography of Native American rodeo. A close friend of the family was an artist, a sculptor who had attended the Institute of American Indian Arts in Santa Fe, then returned home to raise his family on the reservation. One afternoon, this friend came by the house and asked me to accompany him on the three-hour drive south to Sedona, a small resort town where several galleries specialized in Native American art. One of the galleries had bought his work before, and he was hoping to sell a couple more sculptures in order to raise some cash. We walked over to his makeshift outdoor studio, bundled four large alabaster sculptures in flannel sheets and tied them to the bed of his pickup truck, then set off down the sandy road to the highway (see fig. I.1).

The sculptures were stylized depictions of Navajo men and women holding sheep, baskets, and cradleboards, typical of my friend's work and similar to the carvings he had previously sold to art dealers. In Sedona, we unloaded the truck and dragged his heavy stones into a gallery. The owner, a blond woman wearing a thick Navajo turquoise-and-silver necklace, contemplated my friend, who was dressed in a long-sleeve flannel shirt and Wrangler jeans and whose dark hair was streaked with fine, white alabaster dust, and then his sculptures, also covered with dust, and finally said, "Sorry. They're just not Indian enough."

Were there enough sculptures in the gallery just then? Did this woman find the flat faces my friend had learned to carve at the Institute of American Indian Arts (IAIA) unappealing? Was she hesitant to deal with "reservation Indians," most of whom are reluctant to leave

I.1. Navajo brothers Alfred Boyd (left) and Roy "Dune" Walters refine alabaster sculptures in their backyard studio. Photograph by Margaret Dubin

work on consignment because they need cash up front? At the time, no questions were asked. My friend wrapped the stones and pushed them into the truck.[1] We silently shrugged it off, then went to eat at McDonald's. The incident stuck in my mind, however, a clear sign that things were not as they seemed in the Native American art world. As my interest in the subject grew, I started to ask questions at galleries in the Bay Area. Several years later, I undertook an intensive research project that led me to artists, collectors, and galleries across the country. Only then could I begin to understand the dynamics of this art world, in which objects serve as symbols of culture and mediators of complex negotiations over ethnic identity, political power, and social status.

■

Throughout this century, interest in Native American people and their products has accompanied aesthetic trends, such as the Arts and Crafts Movement, or political shifts, such as the newfound sympathy for Indian tribes during the New Deal. Recurrent desire for Indian objects created a cycle of cultural death and rebirth by depleting the supply of antiquities, then encouraging the revitalization of moribund forms and technologies. This cycle captured the attention of scholars and sustained consumer interest; it also obscured the larger power relations that structure an art world in which the majority of Native-produced objects are represented, discussed, and exchanged by non-Native people. In the following chapters, I attempt to describe and analyze this art world.

Scholars commonly describe contemporary ethnic art worlds as spaces where power is unevenly distributed, paralleling the inequalities of colonialism. Interactions within these spaces are asymmetrical, with "native peoples sell[ing] special forms of art to members of politically and economically dominant cultures" (Parezo 1990:565, see also Graburn 1976). I argue for a more complex system. By connecting public notions of imagined and legislated Native Americans (chapters 1 and 2) to the processes and politics of consuming, producing, representing, and historicizing (chapters 3, 4, 5 and 6), I generate a theoretical understanding of collecting (chapter 7) in which political positions and cultural identities are negotiated, not preordained by postcolonial formulations.

■

Native-made objects are found in every state of the nation. In rural areas, often on or near reservations, Native American art is sold at "rock shops," pawn shops, trading posts,[2] and sometimes even Dairy Queens. These outlets are frequented by cross-country travelers, primarily tourists on restricted budgets. Wealthy travelers will sometimes seek out these rural stores because they are thought to be "closer to the source," and thus cheaper and more authentic. Some dealers of historic material still make regular trips to reservations, where they visit traders and keep an eye out for Indian families or individuals willing to trade their heirlooms for cash. Many historic collections were formed in this manner, with urban collectors negotiating directly with the Native American owners or with reservation-based middlemen, either trading-post owners or government agents.

It is every collector's dream to find rare and beautiful objects in unlikely places. LJ[3], an East Coast dealer who has been collecting and trading historic Native American art for nearly thirty years, spoke fondly of the day she discovered a collection of late-nineteenth-century Pomo baskets in an attic on Long Island. An elderly woman was moving to a smaller home and was cleaning out her attic when she found a box full of dusty old baskets. Not sure where they were from, she called a local antique dealer, who referred her to LJ. When LJ arrived, she found a group of well-preserved Pomo baskets that had been collected by the woman's grandfather decades earlier and stored since that time in a cardboard box. Needless to say, the owner didn't know their market value. LJ bought the baskets on the spot.

Apart from the occasional serendipitous discovery, new material rarely enters the antique market. Most transactions merely recirculate material from one collection to another. Dealers sometimes sell the same object several times, as do auction houses. Since the 1970s, auction sales have become the primary method of transferring ownership of Native American antiquities (Frisbie 1987:238). Many dealers attend the two major auctions of Native American art, held each November and May at Christie's and Sotheby's in New York City. These auctions are scheduled only a few days apart so long-distance clients can attend both on the same trip. Dealers who can't attend buy the catalog and a list of "hammer prices," so they can see what objects have come on the market, what their value was estimated to be, and how much other dealers were willing to pay for them. Auction results are also published in the main trade journal, *American Indian Art* magazine, in a column called "Auction Block."

A growing trend in the marketing of historic Indian art is the antiquities or ethnographic art show, where a large number of dealers rent booths to display their wares. According to Kim Martindale, a Santa Fe collector and dealer who organizes these shows, collectors like this format because there is more selection, and thus greater opportunity to negotiate. Dealers also take advantage of the wide selection to trade among themselves.

Like the rural trading posts, urban galleries that sell contemporary or historic pottery, jewelry, and rugs usually specialize in Native American art. Native American painters and sculptors, however, are increasingly represented by contemporary art galleries that do not specialize in Native American art. Contemporary art dealers whose stables include only one or two Native American artists are not generally considered insiders in the Native American art world. For example, a small Connecticut gallery represents one Native American artist, the Navajo painter and printmaker Michael McCabe. The gallery's owner was vacationing in Santa Fe when she first saw McCabe's work, which at the time consisted of brightly colored abstract oils collaged with women's clothing patterns. "It doesn't matter that he is Native American, but it's a plus. His work is very abstract, and it just fits in with what we have here," the owner explained.

Exceptions to this rule are found primarily in Scottsdale and Santa Fe and, to a lesser extent, in Seattle. These cities serve as regional art centers for the surrounding reservation communities as well as major national centers for contemporary and historic Native American art. In these cities Native American art has become part of the regional style, and Native American artists are represented alongside non-Native American artists in galleries that specialize in arts of the region. In Santa Fe, LewAllen Cline Gallery represents more than sixty contemporary artists, including five of the region's top Native American artists. Every summer these artists are shown together, in conjunction with Santa Fe's annual Indian Market, but just as often they are exhibited individually, in an annual schedule of shows that includes well-known non-Native American artists such as Judy Chicago and Roy DeForest.

▪

Anthropologists and art historians have employed a range of strategies to organize and analyze the material culture of non-Western peoples. The simplest approach is the culture-area model, which groups objects by cultural origin. Another common strategy is to focus on a single medium or form, such as baskets, wood carvings, or paintings. When a particular cultural community is known for its artistry in one medium, the focus can be narrowed further, as in the publications on Southwestern Pueblo pottery, Northwest Coast totem poles, and Plains beadwork.

Scholars viewing the objects in question as "art," rather than "artifacts," tend to reject the ethnographic culture-area model in favor of more qualitative categories, such as folk art (Rosenak and Rosenak 1994), tourist art (Graburn 1976), or fine art (Archuleta and

Strickland 1991). The ranking of objects into qualitative categories based on Western aesthetic values is problematic, however, when it fails to consider the unequal power relations that structure the evaluation process. Some scholars have attempted to remedy this problem by expanding their scope to include the consumption and display of art objects within a particular geographical region (Brody 1971). From here it is easy to drop the production component and focus solely on consumption (Cole 1985).

My goal was to link production to consumption by describing contemporary discourses of display and mechanisms of exchange. As in sociologist David Halle's innovative study of "primitive" art in New York City homes, I sought the meaning of objects not in their forms or functions, but in the "complex processes of the everyday lives of [their] audience" (Halle 1993a:413). Because Native American objects move through a maze of mediators in the marketplace, their meanings are negotiable, shifting with the desires of buyers and sellers, the way prices shift with changes in supply and demand. Christopher Steiner paid attention to this dynamic in his thoughtful study of African art (1994), as did Fred Myers in his work on Australian Aboriginal art (1989, 1991, 1994). But within the literature on Native American art, few scholars had attempted to integrate

discourse analysis with ethnography. J. J. Brody's *Indian Painters and White Patrons* (1971) came close, but its subject was limited by region and medium. I was committed to revealing the larger ideas that structured the marketplace as well as the ideological repercussions of marketplace practices.

My research began in earnest in the summer of 1995. Up to that point, most of my experience with Native American art had been on or near the reservations of the Southwest. Already familiar with the modes of production and mechanisms of exchange in this region, I decided to shift my attention to consumers. I focused on those consumers who could be categorized as collectors, reasoning that the information I sought might be more accessible in consumers who specialized in Indian objects, especially expensive objects. It soon became clear, however, that collectors, like artists, were constantly interacting with people in other sectors of the art world, such as dealers, museum curators, auction-house staff, and artists. If I wanted to generate a comprehensive ethnographic study, I would have to expand my framework.

The people with whom collectors interact form a community of sorts, an "imagined" community[4] bound not by geography or ethnicity but by their interest in Indian objects. The system that structures this community is the social and economic nexus of the Western

I.2. American Indian Community House Gallery/Museum. Photograph courtesy of Rafael Macia

capitalist art world. The term "art world," pre-viously used in a casual way to denote those fashionable people associated with elite forms of Western art, was promoted to common scholarly usage by sociologist Howard Becker. In his 1982 book *Art Worlds*, Becker liberalized the term to include people who participate in every stage of art production, from assigning conventions and preparing materials to creat-ing, distributing, and criticizing artworks. Although this approach now seems common-sensical, at the time it revolutionized the study of art by taking the whole system, not just one part, as the unit of analysis.

In my effort to capture the extensive net-work of human relationships that make up the market and influence contemporary collecting, I used Becker's "art world" as the model as well as the larger context in which Native American objects were produced and consumed. Such a broad scope necessitated multiple and eclectic fieldsites. Over the course of eighteen months, I conducted research in such places as the museums and art galleries of New York City, Seattle, and Santa Fe; artists' studios in the Southwest; and collectors' homes in New Jersey, Ohio, and California.

My first stop was New York City, art capital of the nation and home to many private col-lectors of Native American art. New York City is also the temporary sanctuary of one of the largest public collections of Native American objects in the world. Amassed in the early years of this century by George Gustav Heye, it is now owned and curated by the Smithsonian's National Museum of the American Indian (NMAI). I spent eight months in the New York metropolitan area, where I attended auctions at Sotheby's and Christie's, volunteered at the American Indian Community House's (AICH) small non-profit art gallery and at the much larger NMAI, attended pow-wows and "ethno-graphic" art fairs, and interviewed collectors, dealers, auction-house staff, museum curators, and artists (see fig. I.2). Through my work at AICH, I developed a close relationship with Joanna Bigfeather, a Cherokee ceramicist, cura-tor, and professor who supported my research wholeheartedly and connected me with prominent collectors, artists, curators, and crit-ics throughout the country.

After leaving New York City, I returned to the San Francisco Bay Area and spent about three months volunteering at American Indian Contemporary Arts (AICA), the West Coast counterpart of the AICH art gallery. Former curator Sara Bates and director Janeen Antoine generously shared their knowledge and extensive contacts with me. From this location I interviewed more artists, collectors, and curators. During breaks from fieldwork in New York and San Francisco, I traveled twice to Seattle, Vancouver, and various tribal com-munities on the islands north of Vancouver to research the rapidly growing market for Northwest Coast art.

My final fieldsite was Santa Fe, center of the international marketplace for historic and contemporary Native American art. Here I worked as an unpaid intern at Horwitch LewAllen (now LewAllen Cline), where I generally neglected my assigned tasks in favor of talking to clients and artists. To gain experience in other sectors of the market, I also worked at William Channing's marvelous gallery of antiquities, where I met itinerant traders and reclusive collectors, and Leslie Muth's folk-art emporium, where unannounced visits from Navajo potters were met with delight. On my days off I conducted interviews with collectors and artists throughout New Mexico.

■

Disparate sites of production and consumption are linked to each other, and to the history of non-Indian desire for Indian objects, by the complex process of collecting. Collecting, in turn, serves as a microcosm for examining the ideas and interactions that constitute the larger public experience of "Indianness." On a theoretical level, collecting functions much like tourism, which sociologist Dean MacCannell defines as an attempt to "overcome the discontinuity of modernity [by] incorporating its fragments into unified experience" (1989

[1976]:13). The average non-Native American perceives the survival of tribal people and the modern production of tribal arts as just such a discontinuity of modernity. Some collectors minimize this discontinuity with the universalist rhetoric of Western art; others emphasize it in order to increase the exotic appeal of objects. Regardless, the act of collecting allows collectors to resolve discontinuities by incorporating alien objects and people into their own lives, on their own terms. The process of collecting moves the non-Indian collector closer to the Indian artist, but the structure of the interaction forces an essential distance that few have the desire or means to overcome.

As an ethnographer, I have endeavored to present an accurate and sensitive account of collecting and the larger Native American art world, based on extensive interviews, observations, and participation. I make no pretense, however, of political neutrality. My primary concern has been to learn the ways in which the larger art-culture system appropriates Native American objects and artists to its own purposes, despite the often admirable intentions to the contrary of individual players. This appropriation is not monologic—both Native Americans and non-Native Americans participate, sometimes unwittingly and, other times, strategically. Nor is it ubiquitous—pockets of resistance exist where artists continue to create political art they know won't sell, dealers fold profits back into Native American com-munities, and museum curators relinquish control to tribal agents, no matter what kind of chaos ensues. But these small acts hardly dent the larger system, which seeks to control people by manipulating the movement of objects. In the words of James Clifford, "[t]he relations of power whereby one portion of humanity can select, value, and collect the pure products of others need to be criticized and transformed" (1988:213).

C h a p t e r   1

NATIVE AMERICAN peoples and their products have been objects of European curiosity and desire since first contact. As America's only indigenous Other, Indians are desired as they were, or as they might have been, had they not been colonized. America's tribal people are best known, in fact, in imaginary or historical forms. They are conjured as relics of a primitive race, alternately more savage, more simple, or closer to nature than their imaginers. Images of these Indians abound in advertisements, movies, and books, while their living descendants remain hidden from public view, surviving quietly on reservations or in urban enclaves.

Indian arts and crafts are one of the most visible indications of tribal survival in contemporary America. As such, they serve an important function within their makers' communities, encouraging tribal solidarity in the present by providing evidence of continuity with a sovereign past. This holds true even for objects made in borrowed or invented traditions. For consumers, however, Native-made objects often serve an opposite purpose. Where the marketplace separates producers from consumers, and attaches essentializing rhetoric to objects traveling across this divide, Indian products have come to represent and even replace their makers in the American consciousness. Objects replace people, just as the material culture removed from reservations has replaced its creators. Museums are full of objects created by eighteenth- and nineteenth-century Indians who have long since passed away. Likewise, art galleries and museum shops are full of objects created by living Indians who remain hidden, on view only occasionally as performers of culture, containers of race.

In this chapter, I discuss how Western desire for Native American products sprang from the union of America's imagined Indian[1] and the West's historical fascination with non-Western, or "primitive," objects. The material consequence of this desire was a massive displacement of objects, an international dispersal of Native American material culture. In tracing the nature and effects of displacement, this chapter also provides a brief history of collecting.

■

The concept of Indians as imagined or socially constructed is not new. In 1953, historian Roy Harvey Pearce outlined the national discourse on Native Americans in a brilliant book, *Savagism and Civilization: A Study of the Indian and the American Mind.* Prescient of the late-twentieth-century academic preoccupation with hegemonic discourse and ideology, Pearce's study was founded on the belief that ideas "could be separated out of texts and discourses and studied logically and analytically in historical context" (Krupat in Pearce 1988 [1953]). Pearce drew on a wide variety of literary sources to illustrate how the social and racial category "Indian" was constructed according to ideologies that required meek or hostile foils to the manifest destiny of American civilization.

At the time of its publication, Pearce's book was virtually ignored. Today, reprinted in paperback by the University of California Press, it is a gold mine for students of Native American Studies, for whom it is no surprise that Indians are still imagined by the American

public, and that this imagination hinders the progress toward tribal sovereignty.[2]

Robert Berkhofer expanded on Pearce's work in *The White Man's Indian: Images of the American Indian from Columbus to the Present* (1979), in which he historicized the imagined Indian in a structural framework. "Since Whites primarily understood the Indian as an antithesis to themselves, then civilization and Indianness as they defined them would forever be opposites" (Berkhofer 1979:29). Berkhofer analyzed images in literature, art, and science to show how successive configurations of the Indian functioned to validate specific Western ideas. This correlation is clearly found in the New England Puritan world view, for example, that perceived "Indians as well as English sinners as an inverted expression of [the Puritans'] cultural ideal" (Simmons 1981:58).

Throughout American history, perceptions of the West have remained relatively stable, by putting in the foreground civilization, progress, and culture. Meanwhile, key elements of the imagined Indian have varied, at times highlighting the savage, the primitive, the childlike, or the natural. In the early days of anthropology, the classical evolutionism of Lewis Henry Morgan relied on the "current savagery" of American Indians to "fill in the gaps in the evidence of the historical record" (Berkhofer 1979:47). As successive removals of tribal groups reduced the physical threat to American civilization, a more nostalgic attitude arose that claimed the Indian as a symbol of history and nationhood. "[Native American] history is, to some extent, our history," lectured the nineteenth-century ethnographer Henry Rowe Schoolcraft. "The tomb that holds a man derives all its moral interest *from* the man, and would be destitute of it without him. America is the tomb of the Red man" (Schoolcraft in Hinsley 1981:20).

The imagining of Indians has continued up to the present day, generating a stock repertoire of representations for the mass media to broadcast in a variety of formats (e.g., the feature movies *Dances With Wolves, Pocahontas, Indian in the Cupboard)*. Mainstream institutions and corporations use images of Native Americans and Native American products to convey to the public their patriotism, longevity, or affinity to nature. When Walt Disney World built its Wilderness Lodge in Orlando, Florida, in 1994, the company commissioned a pair of fifty-five-foot totem poles from Anglo artist Duane Pasco to serve as a modern interpretation of the turn-of-the-century West. The situation was ironic but somehow appropriate: a non-Native American hired to carve Northwest-style totem poles to commemorate the time period in which Native American communities were closest to extinction.

Contemporary tribal artists sometimes employ familiar images of Indians in ironic or sarcastic ways for subversive purposes (see fig. 1.1). The commercial value of widely recognized representations is not ignored, however, and despite their disfavor among Native American intellectuals, popular representations are often employed to promote tourism to Indian reservations and casinos. Stereotypical images are also used by Native American political leaders to support specific causes, as Sam Gill noted in his controversial book, *Mother Earth* (1987).[3]

Ironically, reliance on familiar images in the political arena can have the effect of desensitizing the public to real problems. As tribes seek the restitution of their legal sovereignty, complex and potentially violent political situations have erupted throughout Indian country. These conflicts occur "beyond the ken of most Americans, for whom Indians largely remain a people of myth and fantasy" (Bordewich 1996:40). During the summer of 1996, for example, collectors lined up on the plaza in Santa Fe, New Mexico, to buy Indian art, ignorant of the nearby protest march organized by Pueblo tribes fighting to keep their casinos open. In this way contemporary collecting inscribes an imagined Indian over political subjects.

■

The collecting of Native American material culture is part of the larger historical phenomenon

1.1. "Big Chief Series" by Joanna O. Bigfeather (Cherokee), 1992, ceramic, raku glaze. Photograph courtesy of the artist

of Western desire for exotic objects. Mary W. Helms traced the roots of this desire to Europe in the Middle Ages, when alien objects were coveted not for their physical forms but for their "cosmological qualities and powers" (1994:357). Objects from foreign lands helped their collectors to organize and understand the "wilderness" that stretched beyond their physical and cultural boundaries. Susan Stewart (1993) saw the same phenomenon in modern "longings" for souvenirs of the exotic. Human difference once conceptualized in terms of space is now conceived in terms of time, with authentic "others" existing only in the past. In Stewart's paraphrasing of Jean Baudrillard, "the exotic object, like the antique, functions to lend authenticity to the abstract system of modern objects, and . . . the indigenous object fascinates by means of its anteriority" (1993:146). Stewart's emphasis on the appeal of cultural antiquity—an object's putative association with evolutionary anteriority—is useful in understanding the value accorded to the racial authenticity of Native American objects.

Desire for exotic objects persisted through the Age of Enlightenment into the early years of social science and the twentieth century. The first non-Native American collectors of Native American objects were European explorers, who returned from the New World with ships filled with curiosities both "natural" and "artificial." Explorers who docked on the East and West coasts of North America often acquired goods from local tribes through trade or sale. Museum curators have considered the goods gathered upon "first contact" to constitute a "baseline for the ethnological study of material culture" (King 1981:7), a measure of authenticity by which all subsequent collected objects can be judged.

Early travelers deposited their souvenirs in curiosity cabinets, a common feature of royal and noble households throughout Europe at the time (Ames 1992:50). These cabinets became the foundations of Europe's major museum collections, many of which are older and more comprehensive than those of American museums (Lanford 1994). For example, the British Museum's Northwest Coast collection contains objects acquired in the late eighteenth century by James Cook and George Vancouver. Most of the Northwest Coast objects in American museums, such as the Yale Peabody Museum and Chicago's Field Museum of Natural History, were collected in the late nineteenth and early twentieth centuries (Wyatt 1984), by which time the engines of patriotic, scientific, and touristic collecting had nearly exhausted the supply of historic goods.

The history of American collecting of Native American objects has been well documented, especially in the context of museums (see Fane 1991 on Stewart Culin's collecting for the Brooklyn Museum and Fienup-Riordan 1996 on the collecting of Yup'ik masks). A more general and comprehensive report on collecting is Beverly Gordon's *American Indian Art: The Collecting Experience* (1988), which traces the shifting intellectual frameworks for interpreting objects, as well as the ebb and flow of the commercial marketplace for Native American goods.

Initial American collecting followed the acquisition and exploration of Western territories, most notably the Louisiana Purchase of 1803, which annexed the great expanse of land between the Mississippi River and the Rocky Mountains. This acquisition unleashed a "tide of instant emigration," as James Fenimore Cooper wrote in *The Prairie* (1980 [1827]). The famous explorers Lewis and Clark were among the first to cross this territory. When they reached the Pacific Coast they collected a Chinook basketry whaler's hat and a Wasco twined bag that now reside in Harvard University's Peabody Museum of Archaeology and Ethnology (Lanford 1994:62).

Purchases or trades made in the course of early commercial ventures, such as the Russian American Company and the Alaska Commercial Company, yielded valuable—if incidental—collections of ethnographic objects (see Graburn and Lee 1996). Individual entrepreneurs who relocated to Native American communities at the turn of the century often encountered opportunities to obtain rare or important objects. Around the turn of the century, a man named Adams Twitchell moved from Vermont to Bethel, Alaska, where he married a local Yup'ik woman and ran a trading company from 1905 to 1916. In the course of his interactions with local Native Americans, he collected numerous natural and artificial "specimens," including the lyrical Yup'ik masks carved for dances he had witnessed (Fienup-Riordan 1996:257).

The rise of the science of anthropology initiated a new era of collecting. Early ethnologists saw Native American material culture as evidence of a prior phase of human history. Side by side, objects from "primitive" and "civilized" societies could be used to illustrate the stages of human evolution. Convinced that Indian cultures were on the verge of vanishing, early ethnologists sought "genuine" cultural artifacts. They were dismayed, however, by the slim pickings in turn-of-the-century Native American communities, the result of loss to wars and early curio hunters. This only heightened the urgency of their mission to salvage and preserve the culture of America's indigenous peoples.

Anthropologists had just cause to fear that American Indians were "vanishing." By 1900, tribal populations had declined from the estimated pre-contact high of 1,000,000 to the historic low of 237,000 (Russell 1992). While no hope was held out for the tribes whose cultures had already decayed irreversibly, objects plucked from tribal environments could be saved from a similar fate. Western collectors disapproved of tribal approaches to art history and preservation: Yup'ik masks discarded after the ceremony for which they were carved, fallen totem poles left to rot on the ground, Zuni war gods abandoned to the elements. While these practices were purposeful and in accord with tribal philosophies, anthropologists and other collectors considered them neglectful and irresponsible, which further justified the removal of objects from Native American communities.[4]

Adhering to the tenets of salvage ethnography, anthropologists sought objects that represented authentic, pre-contact lifestyles. Where there were none, they commissioned replicas, as Stewart Culin did for the Brooklyn Museum (Fane 1991:26).[5] Turn-of-the-century scientific collectors had no interest in contemporary items because their forms were "contaminated," in the words of Franz Boas, "by the pernicious effects of our civilization and its machine-made wares" (1955 [1927]:19).

Distaste for contemporary products was rooted in the same evolutionary theory that underpinned such racialist studies as anthropometry. Just as scientists "wanted to study the bone structures of the Natives before the 'pure' racial characteristics became adulterated by intermarriage," ethnologists "sought to collect the material culture before assimilation rendered 'authentic' traditional items impossible to obtain" (Wyatt 1984:23).

Franz Boas was the first anthropologist to pay attention to the aesthetic qualities of Native American objects. In his seminal work *Primitive Art* (1927), Boas emphasized the universal proclivity of human beings to create aesthetically pleasing objects. Even if these objects were not "beautiful" to the Western eye, they were nonetheless products of an aesthetic vision that was as valid as that of any other culture. Hidden in the valorizing discourse of cultural relativism, however, was the disturbing double standard of cultural primitivism, revealed in the persistent anthropological critique of commodified forms. In her *Social Life of the Navajo Indians*, anthropologist Gladys Reichard declared that the Navajo art of weaving had been destroyed by the demands of the marketplace. "[D]esigns have become so complex as to be distinctly ugly. The so-called *yeibitcai* blankets, that is, those imitating sand-paintings, are . . . the lowest in the process of degeneration" (1928:8). Unfortunately, she noted, commercial demand for the *yeibitcai* rugs was so great that traders encouraged their manufacture (1928:9).

The marketplace demands Reichard and Boas disdained were a consequence of increased contact between Native and non-Native peoples, primarily through tourism. As early as 1880, Native Americans took advantage of the otherwise bleak colonial situation by making replicas and miniature versions of traditional arts for sale to non-scientific, or "amateur," collectors (see Howard and Pardue 1996 on Fred Harvey and tourist arts in the Southwest, Lee 1991 on Native Alaskan arts, Linn 1990 on California Native American basketry, and Wyatt 1984 on Northwest Coast arts). For ease of manufacture and increased cross-cultural appeal, many of the objects made for tourists departed from traditional designs and forms (see fig. 7.2). While these changes posed a problem for anthropologists, they were welcomed by tourists. In most cases, tourists sought a different kind of authenticity from ethnologists, one that provided proof (and remembrance) of interracial contact, rather than continuity with pre-contact aesthetic standards. As Molly Lee reports, late-nineteenth- and early-twentieth-century tourists were satisfied with replicas of totem poles, as long as they were made by genuine Natives of the region (1991:8).

Academic disdain for tourist art was supported to some extent by the circumstances of production and consumption. As Wyatt points out for the Northwest Coast region, tourism tended to encourage art of inferior quality because tourists were "less sophisticated and much less discriminating" than museums or local tribal patrons. Tourists expected to find objects that were primitive, even "grotesque," especially after reading the hyperbolic travel literature. In a 1912 Alaska Steamship Company brochure, potential customers were lured with the opportunity to purchase "crude gropings toward art by a primitive people" (in Wyatt 1984:23).

The history of collecting bears witness to centuries of American (and European) imagining, especially in the overwhelming professional and popular preference for racially or culturally authentic goods. Desire to collect Indian objects arose in part from the assumption that Indians were a dying race. Ironically, the profusion of new Indian products generated by increased public demand contradicted this assumption. Most early-twentieth-century collectors failed to notice this irony, the "discrepancy between their assumption and the burgeoning number of Indian goods being handled by traders and curio dealers" (Gordon 1988:8).

Around the turn of the century, the Arts and Crafts Movement intensified demand for Native American products with its rejection of mass-produced objects in favor of handmade goods, especially American Indian crafts. Dealers wanting to capitalize on the rapidly growing anti-industrial movement claimed that "by procuring the work of these 'more simple' folk, one could become closer to nature" (Linn 1990:128). But, as anthropologists pointed out, much of the work was already being transformed by the demands of the marketplace. Dealers resolved this problem by employing a rhetoric that assured the racial purity of objects while encouraging select stylistic and materialistic innovations (see Cohodas 1992). As long as essential semantic qualities persisted, innovations that made a product more marketable were encouraged. At the 1931 Exposition of Indian Tribal Art in New York City, for example, patrons praised the "new bright colors of Hopi and Jicarilla basketry" but discouraged the use of invented symbols (Mullin 1992:405).

This expansion of the market to include made-for-market items of various qualities raised the status and price of pre-contact objects, which by the early twentieth century were collected primarily by museums and wealthy connoisseurs. It was in this rarefied area of pre-contact and early contact-era objects that museum and ethnological collecting converged with private collecting. Despite the competition for pre-contact objects, a limited cooperation ensued, with dealers referring to anthropologists as the experts on cultural authenticity and ethnologists relying on dealers for access to rare objects (Graburn and Lee 1996).[6] Even though scholars maintained an attitude of elitism toward unscientific and/or for-profit collecting, their cooperation with commercial collectors fostered a dialogue that institutionalized the privileging of cultural authenticity over other qualities.[7]

Intense scientific and private collecting resulted in a massive displacement of objects from Native American communities. "As for blankets with old designs," wrote Reichard, "more can be found in New York than on the reservation" (1928:8). In 1930, Boas noted that while potlatch speeches were still being delivered in Fort Rupert, the carved wooden bowls he had seen there forty-five years earlier were gone: "They are in the museums in New York and Berlin!" (in Cole 1985:xiii). These absences further justified prior displacements because they provided "proof" of the death of Native American cultures.[8] They also moved the locus of collecting from the field to the foyers of upscale galleries and auction houses. Art historian Ruth Phillips accurately summed up the situation when she commented that collecting no longer meant a "trip through the wilds of frontier America, but a trip to New York City, to Sotheby's or Christie's" (1995b).

In the wake of this displacement, especially as tribal souvenirs reached wider audiences and objects originally collected for scientific purposes moved into the marketplace, the discourse on Native American material culture underwent a fundamental shift. Once strictly "about" artifacts and specimens, it began to be "about" art. A number of factors contributed to this change, including Boasian universalism, which expanded Western art connoisseurship to include objects produced by "ethnic" or "primitive" peoples, and the unforeseen interest of elite Western artists in "primitive" objects. Edmund Carpenter recalled how George Gustav Heye sold some Yup'ik masks (which he had acquired from the above-mentioned Adams Twitchell) to the surrealist artists André Breton and Max Ernst, primarily through the New York City dealer Julius Carlebach (Carpenter 1991). The surrealists were struck by the raw, expressive qualities of the masks. They referred to the masks as "primitive *art*," and they denied harboring any of the more banal nostalgic or romantic feelings toward American Indians. As Adolph Gottlieb wrote in 1943,

> That these demonic and brutal images fascinate us today is not because they are exotic nor do they make us nostalgic for a past which seems enchanting because of its remoteness. On the contrary, it is the immediacy of their images that draws us irresistibly to the fancies and superstitions, the fables of savages and the strange beliefs that were so vividly articulated by primitive man. (in Varnedoe 1984:624)

But attention from elite Western artists failed to rupture the primitivist narrative. Nor did the classificatory shift from artifact to art elevate the status of impure products, which were even more sternly relegated to the category of tourist art.[9] As art historians entered the discourse on Native American material culture, scientific preferences were translated into aesthetic preferences, with objects still the center of attention and cultural authenticity still the criterion of value. As *objets d'art*, worthy of display in the studios of famous artists (see the photograph of Yup'ik masks in André Breton's Paris home, reprinted in Fienup-Riordan 1996:270), Native American objects were still the containers of race. Picasso's declaration about African masks and sculptures could just as well have been made about Native American art: "Everything I need to know about Africa is in these objects" (quoted in Halle 1993b:246).

■

To collectors of Washo baskets, there is no better provenance than a tag from Abe Cohn's Emporium in Carson City, Nevada, and if the name on that tag is Dat-so-la-lee, the basket's price . . . can climb to six figures. . . . During the years between 1895 and 1935, Dat-so-la-lee and her fellow Washo weavers created some of the most important and beautiful baskets in the history of American Indian art. Non-Indians had taken over their tribal lands near Lake Tahoe, and weaving baskets for these Americans seemed to be a good source of new income. As the years went by, in order to keep pace with the demands of the discriminating collectors who bought these baskets, the work became more sophisticated and intricate ...

> —*Tribal art specialist Jim Haas*
> *(Butterfield and Butterfield 1996)*

Throughout this commentary on the collecting of California Indian basketry, a crucial element of the collecting process has been erased, as it has been erased from a century of academic and public discourse: relations of power and their violent consequences. This is not surprising. It is easy to exclude politics when discussing art—the topics have different languages, the former belonging to real relations between people, the latter belonging to the abstract realm of high culture. But there is a practical reason for the exclusion of politics, and this is the impossibility of reconciling American desire for Native American products with the country's institutionalized violence and discrimination against Native American people.

The myopic focus on authenticity as defined by a contact-era "baseline" was accompanied by a marked disinterest in living Indians. Not only were pure products often more "authentic" than their living owners, but they were more portable, scientific souvenirs that could be transported back to the safety of museum basements for study. Further justification for the exclusion of living peoples from scientific studies was provided by the federal government's policy of assimilation. Heralded by the General Allotment Act of 1887, assimilation policy stressed the timely integration of tribal peoples into mainstream American society (see Pevar 1992). During this process, Native American cultural practices—including arts and crafts—would be discarded in favor of American cultural practices.[10] Working under the assumption that this policy was appropriate and would be effective, many ethnologists ignored living peoples and their contemporary art forms. As Nelson Graburn and Molly Lee pointed out, Boas's collection of Northwest Coast objects for the American Museum of Natural History was more representative of the curator's scientific ideology than of the realities of Northwest Coast people, who were "already well enmeshed in the world system" (1996:16).

But the system that approved of authentic Indian products also firmly rejected Indians. As Martha Menchaca demonstrated in her study of discrimination against Hispanics in the United States, the federal government officially considered Indians an "inferior race" between the years 1848–1947 (Menchaca 1993). In 1913, New Mexico's supreme court denied Pueblo Indians the right to U.S. citizenship, explaining that they were an "inferior people." Previously Pueblo Indians had enjoyed more legal privileges than other tribes on the basis of "generations of Spanish cultural indoctrination [that] had uplifted their race" (Menchaca 1993:590). When the court rescinded these privileges, it issued the following statement:

> The people of the pueblos, although sedentary rather than nomadic in their inclinations, and disposed to peace and industry, are nevertheless Indians in race, customs, and domestic government. Always . . . adhering to primitive modes of life, largely influenced by superstition and fetishism [sic], and chiefly governed according to the crude customs inherited from their ancestors, they are essentially a simple, uninformed and inferior people. (*United States v. Sandoval* 1913 in Menchaca 1993:591)

While all Native Americans were granted citizenship in 1924, discrimination has continued. Within the art world, the mere absence of tribal people from the ranks of tastemakers (Mullin 1992:407, Rushing 1994a:28) indicates a significant imbalance of power. The rise of multiculturalism in the arts has not necessarily aided the cause of living Indian artists; as Cherokee painter Kay WalkingStick explained, "[c]urators have . . . used issues such as gender or ethnicity as an opportunity to show artists who may then be left out of ex-

hibitions dealing with more mainstream themes" (1992:15).

Since the mid-1980s, a new consciousness has emerged among certain Native American and non-Native American scholars and lawmakers regarding the connection between tribal objects and tribal sovereignty. In this consciousness, historical collecting practices that had been viewed as necessary (from a salvage-ethnography point of view), appropriate, or at least harmless, are now deemed hostile and immoral, if not illegal. For example, turn-of-the-century scientific collecting is referred to as a "slaughter of culture" in a manuscript authored by three Native American scholars (Hilden, Huhndorf, and Kalafatic 1995:15). George Gustav Heye's legendary removal of burial goods from an abandoned scaffold on the Northern Plains is likened to rape (Bear Claw 1995). And the turn-of-the-century removal of Zuni war gods from their open-air shrines without the permission of tribal members is considered theft (Ferguson and Eriacho 1990).

Battlefield provenance is considered most offensive, despite the fact that many public collections can be traced to the so-called "Indian Wars." Soldiers were notorious for helping themselves to souvenirs from the battlefield, which they later sold to museums or private collectors. In one documented example, a lieutenant "walked the field methodically to gather nearly one hundred objects" after a battle in 1855 that destroyed Lakota and Cheyenne camps in northwestern Nebraska (Lanford 1995:65). These particular objects, as well as those collected by Heye, are now in the collection of the Smithsonian Institution, most of which is housed at the new National Museum of the American Indian (NMAI) in New York City.[11]

One result of the new consciousness is that tribal groups whose objects were collected under such circumstances are now entitled to compensation under U.S. law. The Native American Graves Protection and Repatriation Act (NAGPRA or PL 101-601), passed by Congress in 1990, bans trade in funerary objects, sacred objects, and objects of cultural patrimony, and requires the repatriation of such objects from federally funded museum collections (see Weiner 1995). The legal justification for this legislation is that certain items belong to the entire tribe and are essential to the continuance of that tribe's traditions. Because these objects are not individually owned, they cannot be bought or sold by individuals.

Federal legislation also restricts trade in prehistoric objects. Under the Archaeological Resources Protection Act of 1979, objects originating from federal or tribal lands cannot be traded or sold. This has fueled an underground market for prehistoric pottery. It has also encouraged the production of fakes. Another federal law that affects the Native American art world is the Migratory Game Bird Act, which prohibits the trade or sale of any object made with the feathers of protected bird species. This regulation has restricted the trade in Lakota feather headdresses, or war bonnets, most of which are made with eagle feathers.[12]

While many dealers and collectors support this legislation in principle, enforcement is a major source of contention among dealers, many of whom have watched their salable inventories virtually disappear in the past few years. Members of the Antique Tribal Art Dealers Association (ATADA) were horrified when Scottsdale trader Richard Corrow was sentenced to five years probation and 100 hours of community service after being convicted of illegally selling Navajo ceremonial masks. This case, the first prosecution under the criminal provisions of NAGPRA, was tried in Albuquerque in April 1996. Despite its distance from the reservation, the trial was well-attended by Navajo people. During the proceedings, several Navajo medicine men testified that the masks are part of the tribe's cultural patrimony, and that as such they are not individual property and cannot be bought or sold (Sandlin 1996).

According to newspaper reports, Corrow purchased Yei B'Chei masks from the widow of a Navajo medicine man for $10,000. He later agreed to sell the masks for $50,000 through a Santa Fe gallery. Unknown to the gallery, the prospective "buyer" was an undercover FBI agent. Corrow repeatedly claimed his innocence, saying he was offered the masks "without any solicitation on [his] part" (Corrow 1996). According to Corrow, the entire family of the late owner had approved of the sale. From the beginning, Corrow claimed, his goal was preservation. He agreed to sell the masks only after he learned that the prospective buyer had "the same desire to preserve these important objects" (Corrow 1996).

Dealers across the country shuddered at the Corrow verdict, not for the sake of the defendant, necessarily, but out of fear that a broad interpretation of the law would threaten their livelihoods, and perhaps the entire business. As Corrow complained, "Almost anything can be considered an object of 'cultural patrimony'" (1996).

While all trade in NAGPRA-identified objects is illegal, ownership is a different story. Museums and institutions that receive federal funds are required to compile an inventory of their Native American collections, consult with tribal governments regarding the nature of sensitive items in their collections, and return, upon request, any NAGPRA-identified objects. As a result, many historic objects have found their way back to tribal communities.

Repatriation from private collections, however, is voluntary. In an extraordinary action that has involved museums and private collectors around the world, leaders of the Zuni tribe initiated a campaign to recover all war gods that had

been taken from tribal lands. The war gods, known as Ahayu:da in the Zuni language, are tall, thin figures set in unmarked outdoor shrines, where they are believed to protect the people of Zuni and the entire world. When removed from their shrines and from Zuni land, Ahayu:da are thought to be capable of causing natural disasters as well as military conflicts (Ferguson and Eriacho 1990:7). The tribe's campaign, initiated in 1978 and enforced by NAGPRA, captured the Native American art-world's attention.[13] Several museums initiated the repatriation of war gods in their collections. One private collector voluntarily returned her war god after NAGPRA became law:

> It was a very personal choice . . . I feel good about it, but . . . I have ambivalent feelings, because I feel that this beautiful object is lost to history. Although there are photographs of it, the piece is gone . . . You know, they're set out and let to deteriorate . . . But, how can you deny that this thing was stolen from the tribe? Even though, at the time, nobody cared. (BD)

In a melodramatic incident that occurred before the passage of NAGPRA, representatives of the Zuni tribe seized a war god from the block at a major American auction house. LS, the staff member responsible for accepting the object for auction, recalled being surprised by the attention garnered by this "piece of wood":

> You would never really know what it is, except it did have a very subtle area where the face would have been. It had already weathered quite a bit. And so I took it in with an estimate of . . . $1,500. At the last minute, I thought, well, let me illustrate it, because otherwise nobody's going to buy it. (LS)

This illustration tipped off the Zuni. LS remembers being irked that none of the representatives sent to retrieve the object was a Zuni tribal member: "That was the part that really bothered me . . . It was like, well, I understand, but then where are the Indians?"

Most tribal people view federal regulatory laws as an "important first step toward reversing the cultural depredations visited upon them by European [peoples] over the last 500 years" (Weiner:1995).[14] But while repatriation legislation has been effective in controlling the movement of objects, many times to the benefit of the tribes, it has failed to empower tribes in several respects. First, it removes responsibility from the state, whose violent actions set the scene for the wrongful removal of artifacts. Guilt is shifted to individuals: tribal members who sold items without the proper authority, dealers and collectors who purchased objects they shouldn't have.

Second, it relies on federal definitions of tribal identity to determine who is eligible to make repatriation claims. Third, it perpetuates the discourse of cultural primitivism. By restricting commerce, repatriation legislation forcibly decommoditizes tribal objects, reinforcing the perception of tribal peoples as premodern, and, thus, incapable of preserving or appreciating their own history. The notion that tribal people aren't capable of protecting their material legacy was one of the principal arguments against the passage of NAGPRA and is now one of the major obstacles to its enforcement.

When an obscure collection of Oglala Sioux objects in the Barre, Massachusetts public library was revealed to have originated on the battlefield of Wounded Knee, library members expressed shock but were reluctant to return the objects. "We've preserved them for 101 years. We're not going to just shove them out the door," the town librarian told a *New York Times* reporter (Sullivan in the *New York Times* 1993). Other library members said they "feared the survivors would bury many of the artifacts if they were returned, causing a part of history to be lost." The attitude revealed by these comments is incomprehensible to members of the Wounded Knee Survivors Association and the Oglala Sioux tribe, who have demanded the return of all the objects. Since the library's collection is private, it is not bound by NAGPRA. But even without the force of law, many people view repatriation as the only moral action. According to library records, the man who donated the objects bought them "from a contractor in charge of clearing the killing field where hundreds of Indians' bodies were tossed into mass graves." Nellie Two Bulls, an Oglala Sioux woman whose grandfather survived the massacre, traveled from South Dakota to see the collection. As she told the reporter, the objects brought back powerful memories: "I was thinking about the people and how they suffered, and I couldn't hold back my tears."

Commodities Controlled:
Legislating the Trade of Native American Art

C h a p t e r   2

As COLONIZER, exterminator, and finally guardian to the survivors, the U.S. government has always had a special legal relationship with Indian tribes. The imperialist nature of this relationship has shaped every aspect of the Native American art world, from the evolution of forms to the public reception of individual artists. It has also allowed the state to regulate the Native American art market in ways that it does not regulate other art markets.[1]

Federal regulations currently impact trade in prehistoric, historic, and contemporary Indian objects. Taken as a whole, these controls reflect white America's long-standing ambivalence toward the nation's tribal peoples. Simultaneously hated and loved, feared, and pitied, Indians have refused to slip neatly into nationalist discourse. To confuse matters further, tribal objects have been held to different standards from their makers. Where objects have been expected to remain pure, people have been ex-

pected to assimilate. In this chapter, I discuss federal regulation of the Native American art market as a strategy to reconcile this discrepancy. While the repatriation legislation and historic preservation laws discussed in chapter 1 contribute to this interpretation, I concentrate my analysis on the Indian Arts and Crafts Board Acts of 1935 and 1990 as the most prominent legislation of racial identity. As I see it, the state's focus on objects as the final and essential locus of race is a project inseparable from the imperialist relationships between tribes and the state, and indebted to the discourses of tradition, authenticity, and cultural primitivism.

■

The legislation of Indian identity is essential to state control of the Indian art market. In the process of regulating the movement of Indian objects, and consequently the rights and responsibilities of the owners/creators of these objects, the state has relied on a standard definition of Indian ethnicity. This definition is quantitative, requiring a minimum percentage of "Indian blood," 25 percent in most situations. This means an individual with one "full-blood" grandparent from a federally recognized tribe can qualify for government benefits.[2]

The state also prescribes identity on the tribal level with its "Procedures for Establishing That an American Indian Group Exists as an Indian Tribe." Administered by the Department of the Interior, these procedures determine whether tribes receive federal recognition, thus, the right of their members to receive benefits. As anthropologist Thomas Johnson observes, the rules for recognition are "very conservative and assume that the group has substantially retained its aboriginal social, genetic and cultural character over 300–400 years" (1997:19). According to Johnson, the losers in this process are those groups with the longest history of contact, thus, the most intermarriage and cultural change. For example, several eastern groups have been denied recognition because they have "changed too much."

Initial identity legislation was the logical outgrowth of treaties that granted tribal members certain rights and privileges. But in an era when ethnic identity itself is a valuable commodity (Castile 1996), the state's intervention can have serious consequences, determining not only material benefits but economic opportunity.

Controversy over tribal recognition and tribal membership has peaked with the rise of lucrative gaming industries on Native American lands. Members of the Saginaw Chippewa tribe in Michigan receive annual payments of $18,000 in the tribal casino's profit-sharing plan, so, it is not surprising that the 408 individuals were angry when they were recently suspended from the tribal rolls because of "inconsistencies" in their ancestral documentation (Johnson 1997:20). In Johnson's opinion, tribal leaders were simply heeding the economic law of supply and demand when they decided that "only persons who could prove they had an ancestor on tribal enrollment lists from 1883, 1885, 1891, or 1892 could be enrolled" (1997:20), regardless of the quality of their "blood." Suspended tribal member Willard BigJoe agreed: "This is all about greed. This has split the tribe in half, and it's all about greed and money" (BigJoe in Johnson 1997:20).

Contemporary authenticity legislation in the arts is an outgrowth of the 1935 Indian Arts and Crafts Board Act. Part of President Franklin D. Roosevelt's "Indian New Deal," the Act was intended to help generate income on reservations, where wage work was scarce. Concern for the welfare of Native Americans marked a radical change in federal policy. By the late 1920s, politicians acknowledged the failure of the General Allotment Act (1887), which had sought to disperse tribal lands and governments, abolish reservations, and forcibly assimilate Indians into mainstream society. The subsequent onset of the Great Depression "all but eliminated the desire of whites to obtain additional Indian lands" (Pevar 1992:6). In 1933 President Roosevelt appointed John Collier, an Indian-art enthusiast and a longtime supporter of Indian rights, to serve as Commissioner of Indian Affairs. Collier had already been lobbying Congress for legislation to aid Native American artisans. In written statements Collier stressed "how the native crafts were perishing rapidly over most of Indian country . . . because all connection between production and market was missing" (Schrader 1983:33).

Sponsors of the act hoped it would carve a niche for Native Americans in the competitive environment of twentieth-century capitalism while encouraging "tribes to develop a framework to support the preservation and evolution of tribal cultural activities" (House of Representatives 1990:4).[3] The act established a five-member board to promote the development of Native American arts and crafts by teaching artists how to market their work and educating the public about the beauty and utility of Indian-made products. During its initial years the board issued free pamphlets on marketing strategies, published a magazine devoted to Native American art, and sponsored large exhibitions of Native American arts and crafts, most notably "Indian Art of the United States,"

which opened in 1941 at the Museum of Modern Art in New York City. This exhibit marked an important turning point in the market because it acknowledged and authenticated contemporary Indian arts and crafts. Newly crafted baskets, rugs, and pottery were displayed in modern American interiors to demonstrate their suitability as decor in non-Indian homes, while the adjacent exhibits of historic objects displayed in re-creations of their original ethnographic contexts established a continuum of authenticity (see Rushing 1992a).

In the exhibit catalog's corresponding chapter, titled "Indian Art for Modern Living," curators Frederic Douglas and Rene d'Harnoncourt justified their then-radical museology:

> Many people think of Indian products as worthless knickknacks or as savage relics that belong in scientific collections or trophy rooms . . . [But Indians] are constantly producing articles that reflect the strength of [their] traditions and fit perfectly into the contemporary scene. . . . Many contemporary tribal products can be used without adaptation in modern homes and as parts of modern dress. (Douglas and d'Harnoncourt 1948 [1941]:181–82)

The act's main effect was to establish a market shaped by the federal government's vision of a salable Native America. In anticipation of rapidly increasing demand for Indian arts and crafts, Congress strove to reserve this economic opportunity for "real" Indians. The Arts and Crafts Board Act defined "Indian" by the frequently used government standard of one-quarter percent of blood, and it empowered the board to punish artists who represented their work as Indian but did not meet the "blood" standard. For the most part, however, the Indian Arts and Craft Board Act was intended to stimulate the market, not limit it to a racially select group of artists. Passed during a time of severe economic depression and growing public concern over the government's past mistreatment of Native Americans, the act emphasized aid to Indian artisans over protection for non-Indian consumers. Consequently, the prosecutory powers of the board were weak. In fact, not one case of fraud was prosecuted in the fifty years following the act's passage.

During this time, Native American painters and sculptors were rapidly establishing a place for themselves in the world of contemporary American art. The Institute of American Indian Arts, established in Santa Fe in 1962, encouraged young artists to explore subjects and styles outside their traditional tribal repertoires, and the Western art world finally started to recognize Native American artists on an individual basis. Artists who achieved commercial success,

in particular, were lauded as stars of a new multicultural era in the arts. Unfortunately, the financial success of artists like Fritz Scholder and Earl Biss spawned multiple imitations, some by non-Indian artists.

Meanwhile, a new version of the imagined Indian emerged, and Indian-style crafts gained popularity as the appropriate accouterments to the environmental and hippie movements. During this boom, the market was flooded with "counterfeit" products, primarily jewelry, pots, and rugs imported from Mexico, Taiwan, or the Philippines. Federal law required imported crafts to carry a label identifying their country of origin, but the label was not required to be permanent. As a result, mass-produced imports sold as handmade Indian crafts were consistently underselling the genuine articles. As a Gallup, New Mexico, trader explained, "Labor in Third World nations is considerably cheaper to produce a . . . product [similar to Native American crafts]" (McKinney in Holmes 1985).[4] When a group of artisans, traders, and collectors gathered in Albuquerque to form the Indian Arts and Crafts Association in 1974, one of their goals was to protect the authenticity of American Indian products. Their efforts were rewarded in 1988 with the passage of the Omnibus Trade Bill (PL 100-418), which required permanent marking of country-of-origin on imported Indian-style products.[5]

The five-member federal Arts and Crafts Board, working with a small budget and based in Washington, D.C., far from Santa Fe, home of the Institute of American Indian Arts and center of the Native American art world, could not effectively police the market. Several western states passed their own laws against fraudulent representation, but county attorneys showed little interest in investigating violations (House of Representatives 1990:4). Finally, pressured by a small coalition of artists whose mission was to expose "fake" Indians, Congress passed the Indian Arts and Crafts Act of 1990 (Public Law 101-644). This legislation expanded the powers of the Indian Arts and Crafts Board by simplifying the procedures for prosecution and significantly increasing the penalties for misrepresentation. Under the old law, willful misrepresentation could have been punished by fines up to $500 and six months in prison. The new law punished first-time individual offenders with fines up to $250,000 and five years in prison. Corporations could be fined up to $1,000,000.

Perhaps more controversial than the increased penalties was the expansion of the law to include domestically perpetrated fraud, a move calculated to impact the fine arts of painting and sculpture. The original act had primarily focused on crafts, part of the national effort to "industrialize" Indian people and control the authenticity of their products. The

Omnibus Trade Bill addressed the problem of international fakes. But as the House of Representatives report attests, the attention of Congress shifted in the late 1980s to "problems in the domestic market":

> In the last ten years, because of the expanding market for Indian arts and crafts, there has been a greater frequency in the number of fraudulent sales. Particular attention has been focused in New Mexico where there is growing concern about misrepresentation . . . of Indian artists by individuals claiming to be members of an Indian tribe. (House of Representatives 1990:5)

Billed by politicians as a merely updated version of the 1935 act, PL 101-644 actually emerged from a different consciousness, one that acknowledged tribal sovereignty on the condition of continued racial segregation. Prior to the act's passage, the United States had been pursuing a policy of tribal self-determination, in which administrative responsibilities were increasingly turned over to tribes. Acknowledgment of tribes as legal entities and of tribal members as individual citizens is evident in the language of the 1990 act. For example, the phrase "Indian wards of the government" is replaced with "Indian individuals." More significantly, the 1990 act expanded the definition of "Indian" to include "any individual who, although not a member of an Indian tribe, is certified by that tribe to be of the tribe's lineage" (House of Representatives 1990:2), thus shifting responsibility for the determination of membership from the federal government to the tribes.[6]

Theoretically, this could have eliminated the racial component of the act, if tribes deemed culture or social participation more important than ancestry. But this did not happen. Most tribes continue to reject individuals who do not meet the one-quarter blood standard, and even some who do. Individuals without tribal status are prevented by the act from exhibiting or selling their artwork as Indian-made. This is a serious sanction in a $500-million-a-year market that rewards racial authenticity over all other qualities.

■

As the controversy over Indian identity legislation unfolded in the public discourse, it proved to be more divisive within the Indian community than without, pitting old friends and colleagues against each other and encouraging public name-calling ("witch-hunters" versus "wannabes") (see figs. 2.1–2.3). As a painter in Santa Fe remarked, the Native American art community was split into "camps," pro and con. This painter claimed he had been blacklisted from a group show at a major mu-

seum because he belonged to the "wrong camp." Some unenrolled artists who had represented themselves as Native American stopped using Native American subject matter, which effectively removed them from the Native American art market. Others blamed the misrepresentation on galleries trying to boost sales. Still other enrolled artists clutched their Certificates of Indian Blood (C.I.B.s) and remained silent, fearful of retribution for defending unenrolled peers.

Proponents of the law include select enrolled artists and activists, collectors, and government officials. Geoffrey Stamm of the Indian Arts and Crafts Board defends the law as valid and necessary: "Basically it's a truth in advertising law....The government has a special responsibility to the Indian people. Art is a big economic factor in their lives and it is part of our constitutional duty to regulate commerce among the tribes" (Stamm in Force 1993). Cheyenne/Creek activist Suzan Harjo supports the law, calling it a milestone in civil and human rights (Harjo 1991). Standing Rock Sioux writer Vine Deloria agrees, calling the act "a small step forward in raising the red race to full status as humans under the law" (Deloria in Harjo 1991). The logic behind this interpretation is best expressed by Chippewa artist David Bradley, the act's most vocal supporter: "It's all about sovereignty." As sovereign nations, Indian tribes deserve the

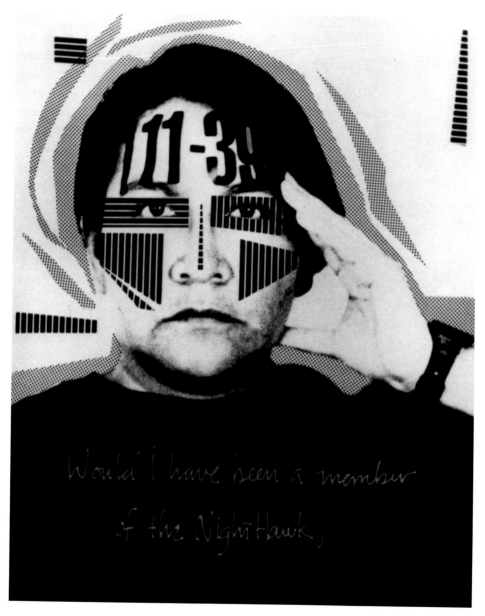

2.1–2.3.
"Would I
have been
a member of
the Nighthawk,
Snake society
or would I
have been a
half breed
leading the
whites to the
full bloods . . ."
by Hulleah
Tsinhnahjinnie
(Seminole/Creek/
Navajo), 1991,
black-and-white
photographs.
Photographs
courtesy of
the artist

Snake society or would i have been

a half breed leading the whites to the full bloods...

11·390

right to determine their membership, and, by extension, their artists. In the absence of this right, tribal identity—a valuable commodity—can be stolen, like so many acres of land.

Unfortunately, some supporters of the act have used it to support antiquated notions of racial purity. One East Coast gallery owner explained how she routinely enforces her own, personal version of the act:

> I only carry registered artists, recognized by their tribe. That's harder with the Canadian artists, like the Kwakiutl, because there's so much intermarriage . . . But in the Southwest, and when you research the Lakota, when you dig deep you find out they're full-blooded, pretty close to it. (JL)

Lined up against the act are such diverse entities as galleries, museum curators, Native scholars, and the *Wall Street Journal,* which, in an unsigned editorial, called the act a form of "racial typecasting" that threatens freedom of speech (1992:A14). Gallery owners acknowledge that the popularity of Native American art in the '80s did inspire some "impostors," but most feel that a federal law is not necessary to protect consumers. This is especially true in the fine-art market, where it is assumed that artworks are purchased for their aesthetic merit

rather than their ethnic provenance. One journalist quoted the unenrolled Cherokee artist Jason Stone, who said, "People can decide for themselves 'who's Indian and what's a rubber tomahawk from Taiwan'" (*Wall Street Journal* 1992:A14). Many enrolled tribal artists also oppose the act, outraged that their community should be subject to regulations that aren't imposed on other ethnic groups. They say the act unfairly punishes individuals who are socially or legally recognized as Native, but, for some reason, cannot or will not participate in tribal enrollment procedures.

In general, enrollment is a good indication of an individual's tribal heritage. But in some cases it is not. Enrollment standards vary from tribe to tribe, and sometimes seem arbitrary, accepting the descendants of individuals who signed certain government rolls and not others.[7] Those individuals whose ancestors refused to sign the government rolls for political or other reasons are generally denied tribal citizenship. Some of the unenrolled could apply for membership today, but many refuse on principle.

Outrage over the government's right to "police" the Indian art market has proven a popular subject matter for contemporary political artists and authors (see fig. 2.4). One particularly eloquent critique of the act is Gerald Vizenor's fanciful drama *Ishi and the Wood Ducks* (1995), in which the Yahi of anthropological fame is

2.4. "Talking Leaves" (pages 5 and 6) by Kay WalkingStick (Cherokee), 1993, handmade book. Photograph courtesy of June Kelly Gallery, New York

brought back to life as an artist. In act 4, Ishi appears in federal court after being arrested for falsely representing his wares at the Santa Fe Indian Market. His savior and guardian, the anthropologist Alfred Kroeber, presides as judge, while Ishi's physician friend Saxton Pope speaks in his defense. "Mister Ishi," Kroeber states,

> has been charged with seven counts of violating provisions of the Indian Arts and Crafts Act of 1990. He sold objects as tribal made, and could not prove that he was in fact a member of a tribe or recognized by a reservation government. (Vizenor 1995:327)

As the drama unfolds, lawyers argue about what constitutes legal proof of Ishi's Indian identity. Ishi is silent throughout the proceedings. In the end, Pope offers Ishi's knowledge of Yahi oral literature as proof of tribal membership. "Your honor," Pope asks, "have you ever heard the wood duck stories? The wood duck stories are heard in one distinct tribe. No one could ever fake the wood duck stories." The prosecutor interrupts, arguing that stories are "hearsay, not evidence." Pope agrees, but counters that this "hearsay" is better proof of tribal character than the colonial inventions of roll books or blood quantum. In the end Kroeber cannot rule in favor of either party. "Ishi is real and the law is not," he states, and despite the fact that Ishi cannot satisfy the provisions of the act, he is an "established tribal character."

Thick with irony and multiple meanings, Vizenor's play exposes the potential absurdity of identity legislation. If the most famous California Indian of all time can be brought to trial for fraudulently selling bows and arrows as Indian-made, then no one is safe, no matter how "Indian." Vizenor, himself of Chippewa descent, has loudly denounced anthropologists and missionaries as colonial emissaries whose writings are the "terminal simulations of dominance, not survivance" (1994:13). By casting the anthropologist Kroeber as judge of Ishi's tribal identity, he suggests a convergence of academic and colonial goals. But Vizenor is not above joining in the attacks on other public Indians, as his other writings reveal (1994:13). Clearly he believes that the authentic should be separated from the fraudulent, but that the standards for authenticity should be set by Indians, not the federal government.

This brings us back to the original problem: who among the Indians is eligible to set the standards?

David Bradley, a successful painter who lives and works in New Mexico, is a founding member of the Native American Artists Association, a Santa Fe group "dedicated to unmasking bogus Indians" (Weisberg 1989:29). Bradley, son of a Chippewa mother and Anglo father, cites the racism he encountered as a child as the inspiration for his present-day political activism. Bradley was born in 1954 and grew up in "Little Earth," a predominantly Native American neighborhood of Minneapolis. When he was five years old, his family was split up by social workers and he "was adopted, along with one of his sisters, by a white couple who made no bones about their feelings toward Indians: They told him to stay out of the sun because they didn't want his skin getting any darker" (Weisberg 1989:29).

As an adult, Bradley has consistently spoken out against racial intolerance. In the 1980s, Bradley turned his anger against "fake" Indian artists:

> When Bradley realized . . . that many of the best-selling "Indian" artists in the Southwest actually had little or no provable Indian blood in their veins, he became incensed. After a lifetime of fighting bigotry, he couldn't stomach the idea that non-Indians were posing as Indians to cash in on the demand for their art. (Weisberg 1989:29)

In 1987, Bradley told a Santa Fe reporter that "four or five of the top ten 'Indian' painters now exhibiting [in Santa Fe] may not be able to prove that they're Indians. . . . These are people making hundreds of thousands of dollars per year by marketing the Indian mystique"

(Bradley in Hart 1987). Despite opposition from the Indian art community, Bradley kept the story in the news by pressuring the New Mexico attorney general to investigate his claims. Bradley's primary target was Randy Lee White, a successful artist who claimed Sioux heritage but was ultimately exposed as a Texan. Other "fake Indians" were harder to depose.

Bradley's vigorous campaign angered many artists and art dealers who felt unfairly attacked. Since the passage of the act, Bradley has assumed the role of watchdog, contacting gallery owners and museum curators to expose Native American artists he considers to be fraudulent (Sprengelmeyer 1993, McMaster 1995). Of Carm Little Turtle, an Albuquerque-based photographer who identifies herself as Apache and Tarahumara, Bradley says: "She's from a large group of Chicanos who decided to masquerade as an Indian and get certain benefits you wouldn't otherwise get. . . . There are a lot of people pulling this scam" (Sprengelmeyer 1993).

Another favorite target is Jimmie Durham, an internationally exhibited conceptual artist who has been represented as part Cherokee. Durham is one of the few contemporary Native artists who has achieved critical success in the mainstream art world. Throughout his career his works have been political in nature, "mock[ing] conventional art institutions and contest[ing] derogatory stereotypes of Native

Americans" (Lippard 1993:62). For the most part, Durham's work has been shown in non-Indian galleries and institutions. Nevertheless, two galleries canceled or postponed exhibitions of his work immediately after the passage of PL 101-644, fearing that a fine might be imposed because Durham is not an enrolled member of the Cherokee tribe.

Durham responded to the chaos surrounding his identity by composing a cryptic disclaimer for inclusion in subsequent exhibitions of his work:

> I am a full-blood contemporary artist, of the sub-group (or clan) called sculptors. I am not an American Indian, nor have I ever seen or sworn loyalty to India. I am not a Native "American," nor do I feel that "America" has any right to either name me or un-name me. I have previously stated that I should be considered a mixed-blood: that is, I claim to be a male but in fact only one of my parents was male. (in Churchill 1992:72)

With careers on the line and large sums of money at stake, it is easy to understand why reactions to PL 101-644 have been so emotional. In the heat of the controversy, however, few have stopped to question the ideological implications of the state's intervention or to ask what it is really about: Is it about protecting con-sumers? Is it about protecting "real" Indians? Is it part of a larger strategy to keep Native people tribal, separate, and premodern?

Considered in conjunction with federal regulations on historic and prehistoric objects, the Indian Arts and Crafts Board Act can be understood as part of a larger effort to limit Native peoples' engagement with modernity by controlling the commodification of their goods. Where authenticity legislation seeks to limit market opportunities to racially pure artists and artworks, rightful-ownership legislation, such as NAGPRA, seeks to decommoditize by repatriating sacred or communally owned objects to their original tribal communities.

The concept of the non-commodity is part of the primitivist discourse, which claims that tribal life is not materialistic.[8] As literary critic Marianna Torgovnick wrote, primitive people live in a "precapitalist utopia in which only use value, never exchange value, prevails" (1990:8).[9] By this definition, tribal art should be fetishized, not commoditized, and any object produced for external markets is inauthentic. In the primitivist discourse, commodification implies biological and ideological corruption. This is the logic that excluded tourist art from so many museum collections (see Phillips 1995a). In the remaining pages of this chapter, I step back from the immediate circumstances of PL 101-644 to consider its place in the larger context of the overlapping discourses of cultural primitivism, authenticity, and tradition.

■

This tag certifies that this product is an authorised facsimile of a carving by Henry Robertson of the Kemano Indian Tribe of British Columbia. Warning: Copies may not be made without the artist's consent.
—*Card attached to a miniature totem pole for sale in a Victoria, B.C. gift shop*

In Walter Benjamin's frequently cited essay "The Work of Art in the Age of Mechanical Reproduction" (1968), authenticity refers to an original that is copied, mechanically or otherwise. "The presence of the original," Benjamin wrote, "is the prerequisite to the concept of authenticity" (1968:222). In this usage, the authentic object is marked by age and experience: "The authenticity of a thing is the essence of all that is transmissible from its beginning, ranging from its substantive duration to its testimony to the history which it has experienced" (1968:223). Copies (e.g., posters that reproduce famous Impressionist paintings) lose the aura of history because they are new, they have no provenance. No longer singular or original, copies are less valuable but more accessible than the original.

In the Western fine-arts market, attribution to a specific artist is a leading component of an object's authenticity, which, along with condition and rarity, determines value. Because authenticity is often difficult to ascertain, the New York auction houses employ different kinds of attributions to limit their liability for authenticity. Degrees of certainty in attribution are indicated by slight differences in the way works are labeled. At Christie's, for example, the label "Pablo Picasso" means the work is "in Christie's opinion a work by the artist." Information regarding the history of ownership, or provenance, as well as exhibition and publication of the work, supports the attribution. In some cases, an expert is quoted to confirm the authorship of the work. The label "Attributed to Pablo Picasso" is less certain, meaning the piece "may be the work of the artist." The wording here is crucial, because authorship is the primary determinant of value. Works with hesitant attributions are not guaranteed by the auction house and are thus less valuable. "After Pablo Picasso" indicates the work is a copy created by another artist in the style of Picasso (Christie's New York 1995:9).

As former director of the Metropolitan Museum of Art Thomas Hoving wrote in his memoir *False Impressions*, art objects have been copied for centuries, often with honorable intentions. Around the turn of the century, however, increasing demand encouraged the production of artworks whose age, authorship, material, or cultural origin was deliberately forged. Criminal forgery became so prevalent that in 1924, London's Royal Academy sponsored an exhibition of fakes as a "primer for how not to get stung" (Hoving 1996:84).[10] To this day, fine-art forgery continues to be a profitable industry.

Tribal arts are also forged, but not in the same way as Western fine arts. Because the art-culture system regards tribal arts as the products of cultural or ethnic groups, not individuals, fraudulence in tribal art refers not to forged authorship but to phony age or cultural origin. At the New York City auction houses, tribal objects are warranted not for their authorship but for their age and ethnic origin, which together constitute their "primitiveness," thus, their value. Native American objects are identified as coming from a particular tribe or region of the country. Typical warranty labels in auction catalogs for Native American art are "A Micmac Card Case," "A Great Lakes Bag," and "A Navajo Rug."

In the world of tribal art, Benjamin's "original" is no longer an individual artwork, but a collective tribal style that flourished some time in the past. His "essence" of history and experience becomes an aura of alterity. Authentic tribal objects are old and racially pure, born before the era of colonial intervention and miscegenation. They are pre-capitalist, made for internal use only. And they are endowed with spiritual power because they have been used for premodern purposes—in the romantic termi-

nology of the ethnic art world, they have been "danced."

Collectors of African art are especially concerned about authenticity, as well they should be, because forgery is more prevalent in African art than in any other kind of ethnic art (Lemann 1987:24). According to Nicholas Lemann, a reporter who investigated the African art market in New York City, more than 90 percent of what "runners"[11] sell is inauthentic "in the sense that it is made to look as if it had been used in traditional tribal religious ceremonies although it never really was" (ibid.). Here, authenticity has little to do with authorship, and everything to do with use. Susan Vogel, former director of the Museum for African Art in New York City, elaborates:

> Authenticity in African art is specially defined; the fact of having been made by Africans is not sufficient to make an object "real;" the consensus is that only a work made for traditional use and actually used can be considered authentic. (1988:4)

Because African objects were initially desired by Western collectors for their spiritual power, evidence of wear is an important component of their authenticity. Masks that have been danced "many, many times will gradually show wear, sweat-staining, and acquire a dark, shiny patina," explained Frank Norick, an anthropologist who assembled an exhibit of fake and genuine African sculpture at the Phoebe Apperson Hearst Museum of Anthropology in 1995. In this exhibit, fakes were identified by their unnatural patina (indicating forged use), unusually large size (indicating modern production for an external market), or unknown cultural function. In order to be labeled "authentic," objects had to conform to ethnographic standards: they had to be made for internal use, and they had to be "danced," or used.[12]

In the Native American art world, value turns less on use than on fidelity to traditional tribal forms and styles. Replicas, for example, are differentiated from tourist art, the former being valued for their adherence to tradition despite their non-use, the latter devalued for its evidence of external influence. The actual hierarchy of value is complex, of course, tied to age as well as tradition.

Forgery does exist, but it refers less to age and use than to the appropriation of tribal styles by non-tribal artists. Controversy over "fake" kachinas flared in early 1994, after the Hopi tribe learned that five New Mexico factories employing Navajo workers were churning out hundreds of dolls a day for sale to tourists, who in some instances were led to believe they were purchasing "real" Hopi kachinas. The carvings were "fake" on several levels. First, they were largely machine-made,

which according to the Indian Arts and Crafts Board Act makes them inauthentic. Second, they were produced by Navajos in Hopi tribal styles, a practice some Hopis consider "cultural robbery" (Shaffer and Donovan 1994:A11). Transgression of tribal styles or traditions happens frequently, and is not prohibited by any state or federal law. Nevertheless, Hopis consider this the more egregious offense because not only is it "robbery" but it is an appropriation of the sacred for profit. As one Hopi man said, "Our spiritual realm is being tampered with" (Ferrell Secakuku in Shaffer and Donovan 1994:A11). But, as numerous non-Hopis have pointed out, kachinas carved for sale by Hopis are also inauthentic, because they have not been used in ceremonies. In this sense, Hopi carvers are also guilty of appropriation of the sacred for profit.

Appropriation of tribal styles or designs by non-tribal artists is a recurrent phenomenon (as is the appropriation of non-tribal styles by tribal artists). Whether the appropriation is offensive and/or illegal seems to depend on where and how it occurs, and by whom. The most clear-cut case is the non-Indian artist who suggests he has tribal heritage. This is both offensive and illegal.[13] Many non-Indian artists produce works that refer to tribal aesthetics, however, and do not claim Native heritage. In the Northwest Coast, several Anglos who work in tribal styles are recognized as master carvers by their tribal peers. "They [the Anglo carvers] are drawn into the tribe, accepted, like blood brothers," explained an employee of Northwest Native Expressions, a small gallery in Port Townsend, Washington, that is owned by the Jamestown S'Klallam tribe. A tribal member who managed another of the tribe's art galleries said she knew some people were offended that the shop carried works by Anglo artists Loren White, Bill Holm, Duane Pasco, and Dale Faulstich, but that these men were recognized as fine artists. Holm, she said, "has an Indian spirit," and Pasco is "more Native than most of the Natives."[14] As David Bradley's aforementioned comments indicate, the Northwest Coast attitude toward transcultural aesthetic appropriation is decidedly more tolerant than the attitude that prevails in other parts of Indian country, especially the Southwest.

At the center of the controversy are a number of questions that are difficult to answer, although many people have tried. Do tribal nations still have recognizable aesthetics in this age of modernization and global homogenization? If so, what are they? Who owns them? And how are they linked to tradition?[15] As James Clifford explains, "We can't assume that cultural change equals cultural death." But "translating tradition . . . is not the same as preserving it in pure form" (1989:86).

Originally a colonialism intended to separate the premodern from the modern, the term "tradition" quickly joined the rhetoric of anthropology, where it was used to describe the static nature of primitive societies. As anthropological theory changed, and as Native people started to participate in anthropological discourse, the term took on different meanings. No longer confined to colonialist usage, the term was internalized by the colonized, "most often as they themselves struggled with issues of nationalism and independence" (Horner 1990:1–2). As anthropologist Ira Jacknis explained about Northwest Coast carving, fidelity to older designs makes a political statement about sovereignty and survival: "We are the rightful heirs of this tribal group. We are still here" (1995).[16] Traditions are even invented to serve this purpose, using history as a "legitimator of action and cement of group cohesion" (Hobsbawm 1983:12).[17] In the realm of Native American material culture, "tradition" has consistently referred to an object's adherence to supposedly "primitive" or racially pure styles and forms. Objects that stray beyond the boundaries of tradition are alternately seen as poor quality or ideologically corrupt, showing evidence of contact with external ethnic and economic systems.

Scientifically and/or aesthetically corrupt objects were (and still are, for the most part) excluded from the canonical purviews of anthropology and art history. Ruth Phillips, a leading scholar of northeastern Native American tourist arts, wrote about her initial transgression of art history's conservative boundaries. In her early studies, she adhered to the "standard prejudices" of art history: "I sought out the rare and the old, the 'authentic' and the unacculturated" (1995a:99). As she explored museum collections, however, she was drawn to other, more eccentric objects, such as "the beaded tea cosies, the pincushions inscribed 'Toronto Exhibition 1905,' the glove boxes of birchbark and porcupine quills, or the Hiawatha and Minnehaha dolls in fringed buckskin." These objects were intriguing because they "seemed to . . . illuminate briefly the private lives of unknown strangers, to witness innumerable small meetings across cultural boundaries." In many ways, these "untraditional" objects represented Native reality more honestly than the coveted traditional objects. And yet, they were routinely excluded from formal museum collections and exhibitions (see also Graburn and Lee 1996). Phillips argues that this exclusion was not aesthetic but social and political: "objects that displayed the traces of aboriginal peoples' negotiation of Western artistic and economic systems had to be excluded" (Phillips 1995a:100) in order to support the dual projects of cultural primitivism and colonial expansion.[18]

The value system that rewarded tradition conflicted with the commercial interests of traders, who profited from the manufacture of contemporary goods. This conflict produced two distinct narratives of culture contact and change. The first set up the "white man," particularly the unsophisticated tourist-consumer, as an unwitting villain in the tragic degeneration of Indian culture and goods. This story commonly starts with the "coming of the white man," an event whose date varies, depending on the region under consideration. Some authors discuss the impact of Spanish contact on Native products, the most common example being the introduction of silverwork and wool to the Navajo and Pueblo peoples of the Southwest (Deitch 1989). More frequently, the narrative starts with the expansion of the railroad in the late 1880s, and the subsequent influx of white settlers and tourists. "For most Indians in the United States, the coming of the white man spelled certain doom for traditional ways" (Deitch 1989:225). As anthropologist Clara Lee Tanner wrote, "How much was lost in art . . . cannot be measured" (1960:137). Arts that were not lost turned mawkish from the "poor taste of the buying public" (Tanner 1960:145).

The second narrative cast the white man, particularly traders and sympathetic patrons, as saviors of traditional Native American culture and arts.

It was fortuitous that the early twentieth-century settlers and health-seekers became interested in the indigenous cultures and historic traditions of the Southwest, and

2.5. "Mass Producing a Tradition" by Nora Naranjo-Morse (Santa Clara), 1993, installation at American Indian Contemporary Arts, San Francisco. Photograph courtesy of American Indian Contemporary Arts

that the prime entrepreneur recognized their marketability as a tourist attraction. Otherwise, the decline of Indian arts and crafts would have paralleled other elements of their culture, as was true in other parts of the United States where white settlers paid little or no attention to the existing culture or to their aesthetics. (Deitch 1989:227)

Basketry technology survived, according to dealer Natalie Fay Linn, because of the efforts of discriminating dealers and collectors (1990: 130). Tanner claimed pottery "fared [even] better than basketry, for there has been greater interest in and encouragement of this craft from White men" (1960:142). As for silverwork, "[c]ritical judging by Whites at the Gallup Ceremonials and other exhibits has helped to educate the public and to keep the craft at a higher level" (Tanner 1960:144).

Juxtaposed as they frequently are, these conflicting narratives reveal a fault line in colonial logic: objects were expected to remain pure, untainted by Western civilization, while people were expected to assimilate. In terms of the social economy of the Native American art world, market demand for consistency and quantity in production came into conflict with consumer desire for authentic, hand-made products (see fig. 2.5).

The persistence of this ill-logic testifies to the tremendous inequity between the colonizer and the colonized. The "white man," according to Deitch, had the power to destroy, and then to selectively restore. As God created human beings, the "white man" created the twentieth-century Indian, and then he created their art, through selective patronage tied to a profoundly racialist framework.

Chapter 3

I think the romance of the West is still very much intact. People believe that you can go out West, that you can start over again, a new life, it's free, there's cowboys, there's Indians.

> —*Curator of Native American art at a Connecticut museum*

I like the spirituality and the customs . . . Like their philosophy of nature, you know, how everything in nature has to work in harmony, unlike our philosophy, where we have to control nature . . . But I find that I don't remember history that well . . . regular history, you know, the war of this, and what have you, I hate to say it, but I can't get into it.

> —*New York woman who collects contemporary Southwest pottery and folk art*

It's terrible, the way all of them live. It's very sad. Have you ever read any of Barbara Kingsolver's books? It's just . . . the white man has taken so much away from the Indians, and they'll never regain it. And they tried to really destroy their customs, their art, everything, and it's very, very sad . . .

So we support them, and we love their art . . .

I feel that when we're buying this art, we're buying a piece of history, a piece of their culture.

> —*Ohio woman who collects contemporary and historic objects from all tribal regions*

In *The Painted Word*, Tom Wolfe's tongue-in-cheek account of the art world, the author claims that collecting provides the patron salvation. In the realm of contemporary American art, patronage saves the wealthy collector from the "sin of Too Much Money," a particularly modern need that arises, according to Wolfe, from the juxtaposition of two bourgeois conditions: guilt about commercial wealth and desire for bohemian chic (1975:21). In the case of ethnic art, and in particular American Indian art collected by non-Indians, Wolfe might see a parallel condition arising from similar guilts and desires: there is the guilt about genocide, colonialism, broken treaties, and poverty, a constellation of injustices strategically employed in the fund-raising efforts of charity organizations. There is the desire for sensual and intellectual experiences associated with Indians: the experience of nature—the wild, the savage; the experience of a simpler, more primitive past; the experience of the cultural Other. As Wolfe's collectors of contemporary American art temporarily toss their allegiance to the bourgeoisie by patronizing the avant-garde, collectors of tribal art might be perceived to be flaunting their liberal politics, or "radical chic," as Wolfe calls this elsewhere (1970), by displaying "primitive" objects in their homes.[1] By this logic, a Wolfian cynic would say that non-Indian collectors of Native American art are saved not only from their wealth, but also from their race, their connection to colonialism, and their participation in the systems of capitalism and modernity.[2]

In reality, a wide variety of people collect Native American art for a wide variety of reasons. While guilt about excessive wealth tends to be relegated to the middle and upper classes, the imperialist nostalgia that breeds desire for "Indian" experiences cuts across ethnic and socio-economic boundaries. To the extent that this desire constitutes a critique of the dominant culture, it is a mode of cultural primitivism (Rushing 1995:3). As a valorization of the products of "primitive" cultures, it is a form of cultural relativism, or its current expression, multiculturalism. Most collectors engage in both ideologies, unwilling or unable to break out of the modernist framework that separates and stratifies people based on their putative membership in racial categories.

Non-Indians can indulge in "Indian" experiences without collecting art, of course, and most collectors start out with the same preconceptions—the same imagined Indians—as the rest of the population. Through collecting, these preconceptions are mediated by objects, by the art world's systems of value, and by collectors' personal experiences. Collectors who travel to Indian country enter into a dynamic of learning and unlearning cultural stereotypes as they encounter information that confirms or dispels their preconceived notions. In the end, however, the proximity of collectors to their cultural objects nearly always belies the real distance between people from different socio-economic classes and cultures.

■

Contemporary interest in American Indian

objects can be attributed to a combination of factors, including the growing appreciation of tribal art's aesthetic value, which increased its status (and price) in the art-culture system, as well as the national Native American cultural renaissance and the American public's increasing pluralism, both consequences of the civil-rights movement. "As these forces came together," wrote art historian Beverly Gordon, "American Indian art became a valued— indeed a 'hot'—commodity" (1988:11).

Experts cite important auctions in the early 1970s as market "turning points" during which prices for American Indian objects increased astronomically. The first leap occurred in 1970, at the Birdie Brown auction in Phoenix, where Chemehuevi baskets sold at extraordinarily high prices (Gordon 1988:11). One auction-house insider cited the George Green sales in 1971 and 1972 at Parke Bernet (now Sotheby's) as the "point of no return" (LS). At these sales, baskets made by the Washo weaver Dat-so-la-lee fetched the "unprecedented prices" of $6,000 to $7,000.[3] In September 1973, a *Wall Street Journal* article named Indian art as the "second best investment in the United States" (Wade in Frisbie 1987:237). And in 1975, the sale of C. G. Wallace's collection of Zuni jewelry, also at Parke Bernet, "drove the market through the roof," according to one Tucson dealer.

One indication of the increased public recognition of the aesthetic value of Indian ob-jects was the birth in 1975 of *American Indian Art*, a glossy quarterly magazine that attracted popular and academic audiences. The interdisciplinary nature of the discourse on Native American art was reaffirmed in 1977 by the founding of the Native American Art Studies Association, an organization of Native and non-Native American art historians, anthropologists, collectors, and artists. While the "craze" seemed to quiet down by 1982 (Frisbie 1987:238), interest in American Indian art has persisted to the present day and is evinced by strong markets for contemporary and historic objects, as well as a burgeoning public discourse accessible to both academic and popular audiences.[4]

The literature on art collecting is substantial (e.g., Alsop 1982, Halle 1993b, Johnston and Beddow 1986). With the exception of Beverly Gordon's *American Indian Art: The Collecting Experience* (1988), however, few studies have specifically addressed the contemporary collecting of Native American art. Information on historical collections is often found in the literature on museums, the eventual beneficiaries of most late-nineteenth- and early-twentieth-century collecting. The current reevaluation of the museum's relationship to colonized communities has generated much detailed, thoughtful commentary on the historical processes of acquisition (Fane 1991 and Fienup-Riordan 1996).

Contemporary museum collecting is tracked in *American Indian Art*'s "Museum Acquisitions" column. With the recent decline in federal funding, however, many museums have found it difficult to augment their collections. Some have been forced to de-accession objects, sending them back into the marketplace through the New York City auction houses. While American museums receive numerous donations (which donors can use to offset their taxes), Canadian museums have been more active in purchasing historic objects, sometimes for repatriation to tribes (Cole 1985:280). Canadian museums are also more likely to purchase contemporary paintings and sculptures (Clark 1994), although with the support of patrons American museums have started to expand their holdings in this area (*American Indian Art* 1997 and 1995).

Private collecting is much less visible than public collecting. It is also more difficult to critique, especially from the vantage point of the museum, which often relies on private collectors for loans and gifts of collected artworks. The move to analyze museum acquisitions has not ignored the private sector, however, and a number of museums have attempted to address private collecting by exhibiting collections assembled by specific individuals. For the most part, these exhibits have celebrated the idiosyncratic nature of private collecting rather than critiquing the means of acquisition.

In 1994, the Fred Jones Jr. Museum of Art at the University of Oklahoma exhibited material from the collections of ten Oklahoma residents. "Sharing the Heritage: American Indian Art from Oklahoma Private Collections," curated by Rennard Strickland, celebrated the state's interest in its Native American inhabitants while congratulating the collectors for their connoisseurship. Strickland, a well-known Native American collector and a scholar of Indian art, emphasized the personal connections between collectors and artists in the exhibit catalog (1994).

"Dancing Across Time: Indian Images of the Southwest," a 1995 exhibit of artworks from the collection of Malcolm and Karen Whyte at American Indian Contemporary Arts (AICA), was slightly more revealing of the intellectual process of collecting. The Whytes initially collected only "traditional" paintings by Southwestern artists in the Studio School style. According to Malcolm Whyte's essay in the exhibit brochure, "It seemed important to preserve some of this unique art" (1995:n.p.) because tribal cultures were changing so quickly. Ten years into their collecting venture, the Whytes "discovered" contemporary Indian painting. They also started to meet artists, which broadened their collecting interests but failed to disturb their preservationist approach. As Malcolm Whyte explained, "[Our] initial instinct to preserve Indian art from the past was correct . . . [but t]he issue for us now is not trying to hang on to the past, but to *marvel* at the way things are changing" (1995:n.p.).

In what may be the ultimate display of financial and aesthetic prowess by an individual contemporary collector, Eugene Thaw arranged to have his entire collection of historic American Indian art displayed in a new wing built specifically for that purpose at the New York State Historical Association's Fenimore House Museum in Cooperstown.

Thaw, who runs a charitable trust that has donated millions of dollars in support of the arts, ecology, cultural preservation, and animal rights, was primarily known as a dealer and collector of Old Masters drawings and paintings. Discouraged in the 1980s by what he saw as an invasion of investment buyers, Thaw retired. A few years later, he and his wife Clare moved to Santa Fe and "discovered" Native American art. In the decade that followed, the couple assembled "the most significant [collection] of its type donated to the American public since the [D]epression era" (Coe 1995:8).

Museum exhibits of private collections generally publicize elite people who collect elite objects, leaving the small-time and the average behind. The choice to exhibit elite collections is frequently strategic, part of the museum's courting ritual to persuade patrons to donate their collections. But these displays do not reveal the personal motivations of collectors or the physical processes of acquisition. A casual visitor would have no way of knowing, for example, why Eugene Thaw excluded most contemporary objects from his collection.[5] Limited by spatial, aesthetic, and political considerations, museum exhibitions generally fail to historicize and contextualize contemporary collecting, and thus fail to connect collecting to perceptions of race and race relations.

▪

When I set out to interview collectors of Native American art, I envisioned a cross-section of the American population. My informants would be a motley crew with disparate incomes, disparate backgrounds, united only in their love for Indian things. My definition of the "collector" was democratic, inclusive of the Harley-Davidson motorcyclists and retired Winnebago travelers as well as the wealthy Santa Fe tourists and gallery visitors.

To this end, my first subject was a thirty-something Puerto Rican security guard and amateur boxer who lived in New York City (see fig. 3.1). This man had a large collection of silver and turquoise Navajo jewelry, which he wore to work every day. He told me his story, in broken English, over dinner in a Chinese restaurant on Broadway.

JR was born in Puerto Rico and raised in New York City, where his father worked as an apartment superintendent. JR's parents divorced when he was ten years old, and he

3.1. The hands of JR, a security guard and amateur boxer in New York.
Photograph by Margaret Dubin

moved with his mother to Albuquerque, where he learned to ride horses. As a young man, JR earned money by breaking and training horses for Navajo and Apache ranchers. Occasionally, he received gifts of jewelry and sandpaintings from his customers, and once he was invited to attend a Navajo squaw dance. As an adult, JR returned to New York City, where he worked as a security guard and trained for master's boxing.

JR recalled his relationships with the Navajo and Apache people for whom he had worked in straightforward terms: "They are good people," he said, spiritual people whose strength had unfortunately been "drained" by alcohol. In New Mexico, his jewelry was part of a work uniform: "when I broke horses, I wore my jewelry and my spurs, it was part of me. I took it off with my boots at night." The heavy Navajo rings and bracelets were a source of pride, an indication of his occupation and his close relationships with Indian cowboys. In New York City, he continued to wear the jewelry, removing his rings only to box and to shower. But in this urban, East Coast environment they were interpreted differently. His boxing coach didn't like them: "My coach says one ring is enough. He wants me to be more conservative." In the store where JR worked, customers were intimidated by the short, stocky man with six large rings, two thick bracelets, and a neck ringed by turquoise chokers. One woman approached

him and said, "Oh my God, you have a lot of protection," explaining that turquoise was a "protective stone."

After our initial interview at the restaurant, JR disappeared. His boxing coach, it turned out, was angry that we had spoken, and ordered JR not to participate in the project. Although disappointed, I was determined to find other informants like JR, working-class people whose unique personal circumstances had introduced them to Native American culture. But this didn't happen. My volunteer work in galleries and museums connected me with middle and upper-middle class white collectors, whose circles of acquaintances put me in contact with more of the same.[6] My research in the other sectors of the Native American art world required me to socialize with artists, critics, art historians, and museum curators, individuals whose social domain generally excludes people like JR.

If the socio-economic variety of my sample was limited, the classification system used by my informants to name those excluded was comprehensive. Elite collectors, especially, employ a strategic hierarchy when describing the consumer community of which they are a part. As in other imagined communities, socio-economic class is a primary indicator of rank (Bourdieu 1984). Among collectors of Native American art, however, there is another important indicator of status, a combination of knowledge of the subject and experience in the market that I call the level of engagement.[7] In the realm of contemporary art, this may refer to engagement in the social and cultural world of the artists; in the realm of historic art, it usually refers to engagement in the processes of acquisition and identification.

Different levels of engagement are indicated by the categories "tourist," "decorator," and "collector." In the simplest sense, these categories measure the seriousness (a combination of longevity, financial commitment, and intensity or depth) of a person's interest in Native American art, decorators and tourists being less serious than collectors. But a deeper reading of the system reveals that these categories can signify other qualities, such as aesthetic sensibility or civic duty. In some places the categories overlap. In fact, most people exhibit qualities associated with all three categories, sometimes serially, sometimes simultaneously. Thus, the categories are more useful in theory than in practice, although among some elite collectors the labels "tourist" and "decorator" find practical use as insults.

To be a "decorator" implies having only a superficial interest, although the interest may be long-term and the items expensive. Decorators are less engaged in the Native American art world than collectors because their objects are selected for the contribution they make to an aesthetic environment, an environment that may or may not include objects from other cultures. In other words, decorators are not "dedicated" to Native American art. My interview with WF, a Boston collector and dealer of contemporary Inuit and Northwest Coast art, was interrupted by a phone call from a local decorator looking for a "primitive-looking sculpture that was about thirty-two inches tall." While WF occasionally places pieces with decorators, she prefers to work with collectors because they are more appreciative of the "living culture" of the work. Working with long-term collectors is more satisfying, explained WF, because "you know [the artworks] are going to people who will love them."

In a wonderfully rambling book about people who collect antique American furniture, journalist Thatcher Freund (1993) distinguished decorators from collectors on the basis of aesthetic vision. Decorators see many objects together in the context of a room, while collectors are more concerned with single, unique objects. Armed with this information, I pursued the distinction between decorators and collectors with BG, a scholar and collector of historic Northwest Coast art. BG grew up around archaeology digs and studied anthropology at a prestigious East Coast university. His faith in the scientific project of anthropology, especially archaeology, seemed unshakable. All his life he had been collecting objects for the self-proclaimed purposes of study and preservation: "You often see things that you feel should be preserved. . . . I sometimes see something, and I know what it is, and I think it shouldn't be [where it is]. So I buy it and give it to a museum." BG considers this kind of collecting a civic duty (especially since he inherited the financial resources to engage in this kind of divine intervention).

After reading my research proposal, in which I proudly employed the aforementioned democratic definition of collecting, BG wrote me a letter:

> We use the word "collecting" differently. What you call "collecting," I call "decorating." Collecting, to me and to collectors I respect (Emmons, Speck, Rasmussen, Boas, etc.), means preserving and studying a tradition near extinction. . . .
>
> Speck and Sapir studied under Boas, the others indirectly, using Boas as a model. All of them became serious, knowledgeable collectors, especially if you include language among the collectibles. They collected solely for museums, never personally, though they often used household monies to save what might otherwise be lost. . . .
>
> My point is that the real collections of American Indian art are in public museums, documented, thanks to a handful of serious collectors, self-trained or

professionally-trained, motivated to preserve and study.

Given BG's highly specialized vocation, his resolute separation of collectors from decorators made sense. In BG's rarefied world, a sense of altruism and a fund of knowledge separated serious collectors from dilettantes.[8] Money, he insisted, was not the issue: "Some decorator-types have big money; some collectors have none." To illustrate his point, BG described an experience that was probably not atypical for him:

> About twenty-five years ago, I was shown the newly built home of one of the founders of McDonald's. I asked to use a phone and was directed to a nearby bedroom. A superb Haida bowl graced a bedside table. I complimented the host and added: "Probably made at Massett, around 1830." "Massett?" the collector replied. "In British Columbia," I explained. "Oh, I thought it was African."

In the popular discourse, collectors are ranked not by their scientific rigor but by their perseverance in the field, their knowledge of art history, and, of course, their financial resources. One indication that a collector has "made it," that he or she has reached the highest echelon of the art collecting world, is inclusion on the "top collector" lists generated by such magazines as *Art & Antiques* and *ARTnews*. In compiling these lists, the magazine editors look for collectors who are not only passionate about what they collect but also consistent. Collectors who fail to make acquisitions are dropped from the list. Editors claim not to be swayed by a collector's financial assets, but they admit that the "financial resources of most collectors obviously play a key role in what they can or cannot purchase" (J. Wolfe 1996:8).

As an activity that generates social status and cultural capital, collecting Native American art doesn't measure up to collecting Impressionist paintings or modernist sculpture. Besides the generally lower prices for Native American objects, there remains in the Western art world an elitism toward non-Western objects, especially Native American and Oceanic objects, that denigrates their value to the connoisseur.[9] This is one of the reasons few collectors of Native American art make the "top collector" lists. In 1988, Richard Manoogian made the list in *Art & Antiques* for his collection of historic Plains objects, which was deemed by the editors to be the most comprehensive of its kind in the world. Ralph T. Coe and John Hauberg made the pages of *Art & Antiques* in 1992, the year of the Columbus quincentenary. Alan Lobb made the *Art & Antiques* list in 1993 for his collection of Northwest Coast baskets. Lobb's short profile

in the magazine notes the information editors care about most: that his collection is the largest of its kind in the United States, that his oldest basket dates to 1850, and that his most expensive basket is valued at $18,000.

Academic reactions to elite collectors are ambivalent. To some extent, scholars and museum curators rely on the wealthy to finance the purchase, conservation, and display of rare objects. In private, however, the rich are frequently scorned. The label "investment buyer" is employed to denigrate rich collectors, particularly in situations where the collector develops a sudden interest in Native American art and rapidly assembles a collection of valuable material, often with the aid of a paid advisor. The implication here is that the buyer has more money than taste. When the Thaw collection was unveiled on July 9, 1995, in Cooperstown, New York, I accompanied a group of museum curators and preservationists on a stroll through the pristine white-walled galleries. One woman's comment summed up the group's attitude toward the collection and its financier: "If you have enough money, you can assemble a collection pretty quickly."[10] A few minutes later, the same woman clucked her tongue over a case of turn-of-the-century Navajo jewelry: "You can tell," she whispered, "that they polish their silver."[11]

Like the decorator, the tourist is assumed to

have a superficial level of engagement in the process of collecting. Tourists may be genuinely interested in Indian people, art, or culture (and for this reason, tourists are more likely than decorators to grow into collectors), but their interest is temporary. The objects tourists purchase satisfy this temporary interest. In the case of Native American art, visitors to reservations and nearby towns might purchase objects made by local tribes, or objects made in the style of local tribes, as a remembrance of their trip. The objects purchased are generally inexpensive and "inauthentic," possibly mass produced or even imported from another country. They are capable of serving as visual signs of the experience but not as artistic masterpieces with which to garner cultural capital.[12]

Even though collectors take care to distinguish themselves from tourists, there is a touristic component to all collecting that works to regionalize consumption. Despite the fact that Indian art is available in many urban and suburban settings across the country (not to mention virtual settings, where dealers have established "Internet trading posts," such as www.canyonart.com), collectors often prefer to make their purchases "on-site," as it were, in order to achieve a more satisfying cultural experience. Indian people live in a wide variety of places and circumstances, but in the American imagination they are located in an exotic Western landscape that is accessible only through

tourism. One Arizona-based dealer learned this the hard way when he opened a gallery in New York City. With the same art for sale and many of the same patrons, the gallery couldn't sell enough pots to stay in business. "There was this psychology we didn't count on," the dealer explained. "Most serious collectors will buy only when they come to the Southwest. We left [New York City] because we found we could develop New York-area collectors better from [the Southwest]."

The Southwestern cities of Scottsdale and Santa Fe are the international centers of the Native American art market (followed by the growing Northwest Coast market, which is split between Seattle and Vancouver). There, and only there, do Indian products have the spiritual power and artistic sensibility that their collectors want, and indeed need, them to have. Whether selecting a souvenir or assembling a large collection of valuable artwork, the consumer is purchasing a palpable piece of that power, and the culture from which it grows.[13]

For some collectors, the spiritual power of Indian objects resides primarily in historic pieces that were created before sustained contact with the white man's markets, materials, and technology. Joshua Baer, a Santa Fe dealer who specializes in nineteenth-century Navajo blankets, speaks of the "living quality" of his weavings: "These objects seem to be inhabited by a soul. They're alive. . . .[T]hey are not

3.2. East Coast collectors Joan and Steve Fine relax in front of their turn-of-the-century Navajo rug and contemporary Yup'ik masks. Photograph by Margaret Dubin

inanimate objects" (Baer 1996:49). Another dealer told me that historic pots "resonate" in a way that contemporary pots do not. Evidence of use by Native hands—chips around the lip, fire marks on the belly—increase a pot's resonance. But the hands are never connected to a face, and the soul of a rug belongs not to an individual with a name but to a community with a culture. "When you deal with [historic] Navajo blankets," explains Baer, "you deal with unsigned works of art that can only be attributed to a culture. Your appreciation of the blanket is a recognition of cultural genius, as opposed to an individual's talent" (1996:49). In this way, the power of objects is tied to the discourse of cultural primitivism, which reinforces the association of quality with racial or cultural purity.

In accord with this belief, some collectors focus their attention on specific time periods or regions in which they believe certain forms reached their peak. AC, a retired dealer who lives in southern California, is only interested in Navajo rugs woven in the Teec Nos Pos style before World War II. JH, a professor of statistics in North Carolina, buys only traditional-style paintings by artists from tribes located in Oklahoma.

Other collectors (see fig. 3.2) find special qualities in all Native American objects, historic and contemporary. MG and AG of Ohio collect many kinds of Indian art. Contemporary and

historic arts of at least five different tribal groups are represented in the parlor of their grand suburban home. Hanging on the walls are a late-nineteenth-century parfleche (a rectangular rawhide container made by tribes in the Northern Plains), a 1994 monoprint of a buffalo skull by Potawatomi artist Doug Coffin, and three contemporary Hopi wicker plaques. Miniature pots by several different artists sit on a custom-made shelf above a bookcase that displays new and old kachinas and a miniature Yup'ik mask.

The Gs' favorite medium, however, is pottery. Sitting in their living room, they recalled the way they felt when they first encountered Pueblo pottery on a vacation in Santa Fe: "We just got very turned on to it, both of us. It was so exciting, so real, so spiritual, so 'of the people.' It just spoke to us. . . .[So] we started buying pottery." Several other collectors echoed this sentiment about pottery, perhaps because it is still produced with pre-contact materials and technologies. As VM of Connecticut said,

It's so beautiful, and it's all wrapped up in the old lifeways, beliefs. The whole idea of harmony with life, things that you do. Contemporary potters will go out to dig the clay and they will still say little prayers as they dig the clay. It's very much a spiritual thing.

WR, a longtime admirer and collector of

3.3. Bev Rabinowitz, a New Jersey collector, travels to Santa Fe every year to buy Native American art. Here she holds a "dinosaur pot" by Andrew Pacheco (Santo Domingo). Photograph by Margaret Dubin

Native American art who lives in New Mexico and worked at a Native American art gallery, also favors pottery:

[Southwestern pottery] captured my imagination....Part of it for me is the Indians' feeling about the natural materials that they use, and about the historical context in which they use it repeatedly, generation after generation. It is interesting and appealing to me, their tradition of using the designs, using certain materials and not others, of where we go to get our clay, of getting clay out of the ground, even today when it's so much easier to go to the store and buy it, [they] still go out and dig the clay, and have special places where [each] family digs it.

This sense of affinity with the land is important to many collectors, whose collections are their sole link to a romanticized, preindustrial past. "I suppose the feeling I have about the Santa Fe area, and the people who lived there indigenously, and their connection with the land, and the way they feel about it, spiritually, has always been meaningful to me....I feel very close to the land," elaborated WR.

The Gs' urge to acquire pottery is satiated by annual trips to Santa Fe, where they buy from galleries and artists at Indian Market. In between these trips, they read *American Indian* *Art* and *Native Peoples* magazines, study the advertisements, and occasionally ask galleries to send objects on approval. When they need a "quick fix," as MG calls it, they drive to Adobe North, a local gallery that specializes in Native American art. As MG explained,

You don't have to go to the Southwest to buy this stuff, to appreciate what's there. [But the people who don't] are missing something. I love buying something in the Southwest because it's more of a connection. I like buying it more there than I do buying it in Ohio because it's there, and then when I look at it I remember that I was there, and what we did, and what the people are like.

For East Coast collectors, in particular, the journey to the source is an important part of the collecting process (see fig. 3.3). Not only does it provide a structure, particularly for those collectors who attend annual art festivals, but it also transforms consumption into an adventure. When WF traveled to Canada's Northwest Territories in search of Inuit art for her gallery, she was delighted to be awarded membership in the "Order of Arctic Adventurers, North of 60 Degrees Chapter." The certificate she displays in her gallery testifies that she demonstrated "the initiative, integrity and bold adventurous spirit of the true Arctic explorers who have crossed the 6oth Parallel."[14]

The Gs' vividly recall the first time they drove through the rural Hopi reservation, looking for pots to add to their collection. Up to that point, they had visited the cities and Pueblos of New Mexico, never straying too far from their Santa Fe hotel. On this trip to Hopiland they were invited to attend a pow-wow at the local high school: "It was fabulous. There were so many tribes, and we had never seen the drummers before," MG recalled. Suddenly, one of the dancers had a seizure on the gymnasium floor, and MG's blissful touristic experience was shattered:

> It was the most upsetting thing, because there was no doctor. . . . I mean, you're in the middle of nowhere. Nobody came. . . . He had the rattles, the bells, on his legs, and of course as he was having the seizure, they made noise. . . . Finally they took him away. It was terrible.

For most collectors, the adventure ends when they return home. Checkbooks are balanced, a new pot graces the shelf, and life returns to normal. The active period of engagement with Indian people or culture gives way to an inactive period of engagement with memories, media images, and museum exhibits. Some collectors watch movies with Indian characters, others read books or magazines about Indian people and their arts. JH spends this "downtime" cataloguing his collection and attending East Coast pow-wows. AC follows the auctions, and occasionally attends lectures sponsored by local Native American organizations. The Gs' visit museums in Chicago, and attend openings at the local Indian art gallery, where they occasionally meet contemporary Indian artists.

At home, the collector's interest in Native American art sets him apart from his neighbors. As the attributes of the object are transferred to its owner, the collector might begin to see himself as unique, environmentally or politically correct, or at least "earthy." In the end, collecting is about this transfer of attributes, not cross-cultural communication. The experience collectors get during their brief visits to Indian country is generally exaggerated and impersonal. It nearly always culminates in the acquisition of a new object for their collection, which serves to further codify and substantiate their stereotypical understanding of "Indianness."

Artists:
Selling Paintings, Dispelling Stereotypes

IN THE EARLY PART of this century, the term "Native American artist" referred primarily to reservation artisans making objects in recognizably tribal styles for sale to collectors and tourists. As tribal populations grew more dispersed and heterogeneous, and opportunities for artistic experimentation increased, the term expanded—but not without controversy. In the late twentieth century, qualitative distinctions between "craft" and "art" have been drawn, erased, and redrawn; the boundaries between primitivism and modernism have blurred; and the notion that only Western arts convey themes of universal import has been criticized as ethnocentric.

The prevailing interpretation of this condition says that the "pure products" have gone "crazy."[1] The formal structures of the colonial world have yielded to an ambivalent order in which non-Indian traders are fined for trafficking in sacred objects, and tribal artists sit on the boards of powerful museums. But this interpretation is flawed. Just as colonial structures were not righteous, tribal products were never "pure." It's not the purity that has changed, but the power relations, in particular the range of practices and ideologies available to Native American artists functioning in an increasingly pluralistic art world.

In this chapter, I share artists' words to demonstrate how the physical variety of forms in contemporary Native American art reflects an equally broad range of personal ideologies and experiences. Frequent use of stereotypes in the marketplace tends to homogenize Western perceptions of tribal artists, but it is important to recognize that contemporary artists feel different levels of commitment to the conventional aesthetics of their tribes, and that each artist's sense of cultural identity is unique, determined by his or her personal history, aesthetic inclinations, and political or social goals.

To convey this sense of individuality, I have relied more on direct quotes in this chapter than in the other chapters.[2] Statements are organized by themes that reflect what I perceived to be the most urgent concerns of the Indian art community during the summer of 1996, when I conducted the bulk of my interviews. In accord with the current vogue of multivocality, quotes are unedited, uncensored, and—as far as possible for a text of this sort—unfettered by academic commentary.

▪

If nothing else, the label "Native" serves as an indicator of difference—ethnic, cultural, and/or aesthetic difference from other artists working in the United States. This difference is as much imposed by consumers as it is generated by the artists themselves. As discussed in chapters 1 and 3, consumers construct "imagined Indians" to fulfill their own needs. Nevertheless, most of the artists I interviewed expressed a significant sense of difference arising from their personal histories as well as their membership in specific tribal or artistic communities.

It was late in the afternoon when I arrived at Tony Abeyta's northern New Mexico studio, a spacious, clay-tiled adobe room. I had been advised to drop in unexpectedly, because Abeyta was too busy to arrange appointments. Fortunately, my timing was good—Abeyta was in a generous mood because his close friend PR, a Zuni painter, was visiting. When I introduced myself Abeyta nodded, saying he had heard of me from friends in Santa Fe. "Come back with a bottle of good wine," he ordered, "and we'll talk." Flustered but excited to be granted an interview with this well-known Navajo painter, I set out to find the nearest wine shop.

When I returned with a California Cabernet Sauvignon and some cheese and crackers, Abeyta was relaxing on a dusty couch, the only comfortable piece of furniture in the room. PR was bent over a table, scratching lines into a print and teasing Abeyta about his appropriation of Pueblo imagery. The three of us discussed wines briefly—Abeyta seemed doubtful that California could compete with France— then moved to the topic of Indian art.

When I asked Abeyta what separated Indian from non-Indian artists, he spoke not of an inter-tribal aesthetic, but of a shared way of doing things, of dealing with people and moving in the world. He expressed this sense of unity in difference with a humorous anecdote:

> Some people came in from New York last week and told me the rage right now is this installation this guy's got and it's of a pig, but it's cut in half and put in formaldehyde, and it's on view in a gallery. And they took a cow and cut a cross-section of him, and they have him

so he moves around in there, so he can jiggle. So there's some kind of movement. [long pause] Indian people don't *think* like that. We don't envision those kinds of concepts. If we do we're only trying to assimilate, we're trying to be something that they want. And if that's what they wanted from American Indians, we couldn't give it to them. Some can, and some try to, and they do a lousy job. I look at them and say, that's a joke.

Throughout our interview, Abeyta's narrative shifted back and forth between a tribal or intertribal "we" to the personal "I." This pattern of speech was repeated in other interviews with other artists, reflecting the ease with which Native American artists integrated their sense of self with their membership in a community.

Later in the summer I interviewed Dan V. Lomahaftewa, a close friend of Abeyta's. We met at a coffee house in Santa Fe, then drove to his apartment, which also functions as his painting studio. In a room near the entryway, two large, pastel-hued canvases leaned against the wall, nearly touching the ceiling. "Don't look at those, they're not done," Lomahaftewa said. We settled in the living room, a cozy space graced with paintings and small sculptures by artist friends.

Lomahaftewa is a soft-spoken man, thoughtful and passionate about his work. He was born

in Phoenix, Arizona, to a Hopi father and a Choctaw mother. Because he never knew his Choctaw relatives, he identified more strongly with his Hopi heritage. As a child, he spent summers on the Hopi reservation, living with aunts in the village of his father. Hopi traditions are passed down through the matrilineal line, so the extent to which Lomahaftewa could participate in tribal ceremonies was limited. But because his grandfather was a highly respected tribal leader, Lomahaftewa was always welcomed by his relatives on the reservation.

Lomahaftewa's sense of difference is highly personal, rooted in his relationship with family members and the time he spends on the Hopi reservation. As an adult, Lomahaftewa frequently makes the five-hour drive to his father's village. Lomahaftewa also invites non-Indian friends to visit the reservation, proud to share the source of his moral convictions and artistic inspiration.

Angling for an invitation, I asked Lomahaftewa, "How often do you go out [to the reservation] now?"[3]

"Well, I'm going out there Friday, because there's a dance," he replied. "I try to go out there as much as possible. It's almost like my rejuvenation."

During the course of his life, Lomahaftewa has lived in numerous Western towns, but his most vivid memories are of summers spent on the high mesas of Hopi. These memories guide his paintbrush (see fig. 4.1) and gird his sense of identity:

DL: You know, I gotta say, my career is all intertwined with all this history, and when I talk about my career, I can't not talk about my dad, my grandfather, my aunts and uncles. And part of who I am is part of why I paint. All of these continual experiences of being out in the desert, and herding sheep, you know, with my uncle. My memories are like—okay, we're at this real low shack, you know, it's our sheep camp, with a little corral.

M: I didn't know Hopi had sheep.[4]

DL: [Grinning] Oh yeah, you know, people historically generalize all the time. But all of us had sheep, almost every family had some. We had sheep, and my uncle and I would take them out to the sheep camp, and like I said, there was this low shack, this was my memory, usually they have these low, little buttes or cliffs, and they'd build a sheep camp next to it, so they could have one side as a corral. The way I remember it, he tells me, you take them over that way, then you turn over here, and then you take them to the water windmill, and then you bring them back. And he would stay at the sheep camp, working his silver. He was a silversmith. So

he'd be sitting there, he had one of those stones grinding stones, doing his turquoise.

See, that's a memory of mine, my uncle grinding turquoise, doing stuff like that. And then the views, and the things that they taught me all became reality. Things like, you know, part of our belief is that everything, *everything*, has a spirit, everything is alive, everything has a life and death. So, everything around me has meaning. Immediately. And then you look out into the distance, and you see the buttes and the cliffs, and everything is, you know, the stories come to mind, the stories of how they're made, then the clouds are coming around, and they're going to rain, and they are all your relatives, all your ancestors are there, all your kachinas are there, and I remember once, it was described to me that when you looked off in the distance and you saw a rain cloud, the rain coming down, you could see the dark streaks, it was described to me that there's your ancestors, letting their hair down, you know, to grow the corn. That's a beautiful thought to me, so it's like, all of those are a part of my painting, all of those memories, growing corn and listening to my grandfather sing, you know, as we work.

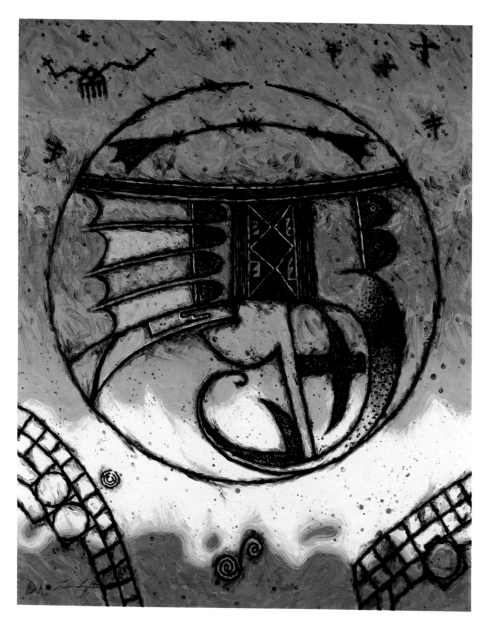

4.1.
"Inner Flight"
by Dan V.
Lomahaftewa
(Hopi), 1995,
acrylic on
canvas.
Photograph
by Murrae
Haynes

Lomahaftewa's sense of connection to a more traditional, reservation-based life is saturated by a sense of separation and loss. Other Native American artists who live in urban areas report a similar sense of separation that is heightened by the physical reality of long journeys between city dwellings and reservation homelands. This is not so much a "living in two worlds," as so many critics describe it, but the integration of different, chronologically simultaneous modes of existence into a single, routinized lifestyle.[5]

Of course, some artists are born on or near their reservations and never leave. Some leave but then return permanently, to be near friends and relatives, and to escape the pressures and degradations of urban life. And there are some who never knew a reservation, or whose tribal territory was not a reservation at all but an urban Indian center that served as home for the children and grandchildren of Native Americans who relocated for different reasons.

Just as an individual's sense of identity is shaped by personal and historical circumstances, the location of an artist's workplace is often a function of necessity. The way artists learn their skills and obtain their materials, for example, can determine where they live. Navajo weavers traditionally learn their craft from older, female relatives who reside within their reservation communities. Many weavers have no formal arts education and little involvement in urban art scenes. Southwestern carvers and silversmiths also learn their skills from relatives or other mentors within their reservation communities. All three kinds of artists use materials available on or near their reservations: Navajo weavers use yarn spun from local sheep, Hopi carvers prefer the soft branches of local cottonwood trees, and Zuni silversmiths buy silver by the yard and turquoise by the pound from their local trader or "jobber," who earns a living selling raw materials and buying back the finished jewelry at low cost.

Reservation artists whose career goals require access to exotic materials, market centers, or Western educational institutions are often forced to relocate to urban areas. In the Southwest, this means Phoenix or Santa Fe; in the Northwest Coast, Seattle or Vancouver. The late Navajo jeweler TY, for example, grew up in an isolated town in northeastern Arizona, where he learned basic silversmithing skills from his parents. By the time of his death in 1996, he was a well-known jeweler who worked primarily in gold and precious gemstones and lived near the resort community of Sedona, Arizona. His necklaces sold in upscale jewelry stores in Sedona and Santa Fe for around $10,000, more than four times the average income of Navajos living on the reservation. When I spoke with TY in 1995 at a gallery opening in New York City, he saw no incongruity in this situation. He was an artist, using his medium of choice and earning a good living through his hard work. His wife was Navajo, and together they visited their respective reservation hometowns as frequently as possible, but, inevitably, they ended up spending most of their time with other Native American artists who lived in urban areas.

Hopi jeweler HL also works in gold and diamonds. But while TY's pieces make reference to conventional Navajo designs, HL rejects the ubiquitous Hopi technique of silver overlay for a stark, geometric aesthetic. HL consistently wins awards for originality, but few on the reservation can afford to buy his work (necklaces are $10,000 and up). HL has clients all over the country, particularly in New York City and Los Angeles. He spends most of his time flying between his California apartment and various gallery shows, museum exhibits, and Indian art fairs. The place he calls home, however, is Old Oraibi, an ancient Hopi village perched on the edge of a mesa in northeastern Arizona. Every summer he gets into his old Ford Mustang and drives to Old Oraibi, where he stays with relatives and participates in ceremonial dances. He treasures these visits and sometimes considers returning permanently, but his asthma is aggravated by the local juniper pollen, and he usually leaves after a couple of weeks.

Artists who are born and raised in urban areas may not have opportunities to learn techniques that are generally taught in reserva-

tion settings. When Tlingit glassblower Preston Singletary wanted to learn his tribe's technique of painting formlines and ovoids, he resorted to studying books written by anthropologists and art historians. Hopi textile designer Ramona Sakiestewa taught herself how to weave, then collaborated with museum curators and art historians to expand her repertoire of designs to include classic tribal images as well as icons from modern American art and architecture.

A few painters and sculptors are self-taught,[6] but most attend art schools. In recent years it has become increasingly common for Native American students to attend universities or Western arts institutions, such as the Chicago Art Institute or the San Francisco Art Institute. But the most popular institution by far has been the Institute of American Indian Arts (IAIA) in Santa Fe, a federally funded college created for Native American students in 1962.[7] Although attendance at this school is not limited to Native Americans, IAIA's student body is primarily Indian and remarkably intertribal. According to a study commissioned by the Institute, nearly all of the 547 federally recognized tribes have sent students to the school; in any given year, sixty to ninety tribes are represented in the student body (Southwest Planning and Marketing 1996:ii).

The intertribal nature of the school's population breeds a powerful pan-Indian pedagogy that saturates students with the cultural, political, and commercial implications of their "Indianness." IAIA's premise is that neither tribal association nor individual freedom of expression needs to be sacrificed in order to create meaningful art. According to IAIA philosophy, artists are the caretakers of cultural legacy: "[J]ust as cultural self-awareness informs and makes whole the individual as artist, so does the informed artist ensure the ongoing life of his or her evolving culture" (Southwest Planning and Marketing 1996:41). At the same time, students are encouraged to "develop dignity and self-esteem" (Southwest Planning and Marketing 1996:39) by learning to express themselves as individuals. This might mean creating images that diverge from conventional tribal aesthetics, or whose primary purpose is to convey a political message.

But the Institute teaches not only art-making but also art marketing, and this is where its philosophy conflicts with the prevailing reality. Within the walls of the Institute, responsibilities to self-expression and tribal continuity are met when students use their "own distinct voices" to produce objects that "inherently convey cultural values" (Southwest Planning and Marketing 1996:41). Outside the Institute, however, students face a market that nearly always rewards stereotypes over individualism.[8]

PC is a Crow sculptor best known for his monumental stone carvings of tribal figures. He studied at IAIA from 1962 to 1963, then returned as an instructor from 1971 to 1974. He still lives in Santa Fe, where his work is shown at a gallery that specializes in contemporary and historic Western arts. During the summer of 1996, this gallery hosted a private party in honor of PC, whose most recent commission—a large-scale figure of a tribal warrior—was on view in the landscaped sculpture garden. Friends of Indian Art, a local collectors' club, sponsored the gathering. Although this was the only club event I attended that summer, I was told that the scene in the garden was typical: wealthy Anglo women and couples, mostly middle-aged but a few quite elderly, swooning over the artist and the artwork, in equal awe of the tall, handsome Native man and the even taller, equally handsome Native sculpture. During the party, PC was available to answer questions. I asked him if he ever felt constrained by the demands of the Santa Fe art market. He glanced around, shuffled his feet, then said, "Mermaids."

"Pardon me?"

"Mermaids. I did this awesome sculpture out of translucent orange marble of these mermaids, but my gallery isn't interested. My gallery wants Indian subject matter. That's what people expect. That's what sells."

DT taught photography at the Institute for a short time before moving to San Francisco. We met in a cafe on Market Street, below the galleries of American Indian Contemporary Art

(AICA), where he occasionally exhibits his work. DT said he "hated" Santa Fe's Indian art scene because it patronized Indian artists: "My students told me how they would go down to the plaza and sell their photographs of Indians for $250, not because they were art but because they were of Indians." NC, an Apache bead-worker who also left Santa Fe, tells a similar story: "After seeing [IAIA students] do stuff just to sell to tourists, I got disgusted with Santa Fe. The last straw was a gallery owner who asked me to bead a Plains robe. I'm an Apache, and I do contemporary work!"

Expatriates excepted, most of the Institute's graduates are groomed for success in the regional Native American art market. IAIA artists consistently garner a large percentage of ribbons in the contemporary categories at Santa Fe's annual Indian Market. Some of these artists go on to achieve success on a national level. The late Apache sculptor Allan Houser, for example, was awarded the National Medal of Arts in 1992. But for many, the leap from the regional, Indian art market to the national, multicultural art market is extremely difficult, if not impossible. The goal for these artists, as for many non-Native artists, is to transcend their local art scene, no matter how lucrative it might be, and "make it" in a place of national or international significance, like New York City. But this is where the demands of personal, tribal, and consumer worlds collide. The most painful

question for these artists is not, "Am I good enough?" but, "Do I have to give up my Native identity to achieve success?"

In her work with Native American artists living in Santa Fe, Apache anthropologist Nancy Mitchell (née Mithlo)(1993) found that artists who asserted their tribal identity had more difficulty entering the mainstream Western art world than those who did not. The Western art world's operating paradigm of universality requires ethnic artists to leave their culture and heritage at the door. "Cultural artists," as Mithlo calls them, "are seen to make only cultural art which prohibits their entrance into the fine arts world" (1993:6). Further hindering the tribal artist's effort to enter the Western art world is the ubiquitous exotic appeal of Native American peoples and products. According to Mithlo, contemporary Native American artists who publicize their tribal heritage are perceived as primitive and exotic regardless of the modernity (in form, content, medium, or message) of their work.

On a larger scale, this problem is caused by the conflicting priorities of cultural primitivism and aesthetic modernism. The former describes authenticity as "purity" in race (people) and form (objects). The latter views any sign of non-Western ethnicity as an inherent limitation because it corrupts the conveyance of a purely aesthetic problem. For art to be truly and thoroughly modern, it had to be *about* art, not about race, gender, class, or any other non-aesthetic topic.[9] (The fact that the art that modern art was about *was* cultural [Western culture] was overlooked by most critics.)

Multiculturalism attempts to resolve this conflict by clearing space for work by ethnic artists (see discussion of the Whitney's 1993 Biennial Exhibition in chapter 7). Undercutting the opportunities provided by multiculturalism, however, are the persistent demands for tribal people to make "authentic" products, the continued segregation of the authentic from the less authentic, and the analogous, state-mandated separation of authentic and inauthentic Indian artists. It is in the context of the federal legislation of identity that multiculturalism begins to look like what some artists disparagingly call "affirmative art action."

The desirability of calling oneself a Native American artist varies with the individual and the situation.[10] Some artists take offense at the label, while others take pride in it. Kelvin Yazzie, a Navajo ceramicist, says he "tries to avoid being pegged as a Native American artist" because he feels the label limits his creativity: "My instructors [at Northern Arizona University] tried to teach me how to do Indian art because I am an American Indian. I didn't like that" (Yazzie 1994).

Abeyta, the Navajo painter quoted earlier, feels comfortable with the label:

I am Native American. What I'm painting, and how I'm working, is all based on Native American belief systems. So fitting into the context of mainstream universal concepts is difficult, because I'm always going to be typecast. I accept that. I take that and I . . . I'm not striving to be a painter who is internationally acclaimed, somebody who shows with Pace Wilderstein in New York. That's not the kind of arena that I've chosen. I realized that there were limitations on what I was going to do as a painter, and where I really belonged. And I find an amazing sense of peace in that.

Preston Singletary, the Tlingit glassblower introduced earlier, gleaned much of his knowledge of tribal history and culture from tales told by his grandmother and great-grandmother, both Tlingits who married Filipino men. For most of his life, however, this knowledge remained personal. While attending the Pilchuck Glass School in Seattle, Singletary produced elegant glass vessels inspired by classic Venetian and Danish aesthetics. As an inhabitant of Seattle, the primary marketplace for Northwest Coast Indian art, Singletary was inundated with the conventional images of his culture. At some point, he conceived of a glass vessel utilizing these images. But Northwest Coast art is traditionally

4.2. "Frog Hat" by Preston Singletary (Tlingit), 1998, blown, sandblasted glass.
Photograph by Roger Schreiber

4.3. "Raven Steals the Sun" by Preston Singletary (Tlingit), 1999, glass. Photograph by Russell Johnson

learned through a formal and lengthy apprenticeship, and Singletary was an urbanite with few connections to traditional communities. So he turned to books written by anthropologists and art historians for instruction.

After a couple years of self-instruction and sessions with Native friends, Singletary produced his first Native-inspired glass vessel, an inverted clan hat complete with carved formlines and ovoids. Next, he blew a glass vase in the shape of a bear totem. His Seattle gallery was enthusiastic and offered him a solo show for the new series (see figs. 4.2 and 4.3). In less than a year, the work was picked up by a Santa Fe gallery that specializes in Native American art.

With demand for his work escalating, Singletary was ecstatic. But in my telephone conversations with him, he also revealed ambivalence. On a personal level, this foray into tribal aesthetics was clearly a positive development: "I feel like I am at the beginning of a long path with these pieces. It is a process of discovery." On a professional level, however, he was not sure how his success in the Indian art world would influence his status as a contemporary American glassblower. He knew only one other Native glassblower, Tony Jojola, a Laguna man who had also attended the Pilchuck Glass School. Unlike Singletary, Jojola had always identified himself as a Native artist, and had nearly always created work

with Native content or associations. As a result, Jojola's work was known and carried by galleries that specialized in Indian art, not glass art.

When the choice to identify as Native is difficult, it is tempting to equivocate, as Santa Clara painter EO did:

> M: I have a quote here from you that says, "I accept the label of American Indian artist." And I have another quote here from you, from the same article, that says "I don't want to be strictly an Indian painter."
>
> EO: [laughing] I'm a contradictory fellow.

Dan V. Lomahaftewa, the Hopi painter, does not mind being labeled an Indian artist. What irks him is the hypocrisy of people who reject their Indian identity in the Western art world only to reclaim it in order to participate in the lucrative events of the Indian art world, such as Santa Fe's Indian Market.

PA, an installation artist, told a primarily middle-class, Anglo audience at the New Museum for Contemporary Art in New York City that he "[doesn't] believe in affirmative art action," and that he "[tries] not to do multicultural shows any more." Nevertheless, PA has participated and continues to participate in Native American exhibits and events.

For artists who don't want to be known as

Native Americans, Lomahaftewa offered the following advice:

> If you don't want to be labeled an Indian artist, it's very, very easy to do. What you need to do is go terminate yourself from your tribe. Then, do not enter any Indian art competitions, Indian art shows, and don't take any grants, any money from the government that has anything to do with Indians, and then, don't move to Santa Fe. And then you go out there and try it, just like everybody else. But don't come around to Indian Market and then tell me that you don't want to be called an Indian artist. I mean, give me a break.

The logic here is simple: tribal identity is not a cloak to shrug on in certain situations, shrug off in others. It is a core element of the self, forged by history and culture, a sign of suffering, perhaps, and more certainly a sign of survival. This is why the fraudulent assumption of tribal identity is such a grave offense to so many Native American people.

Attitudes toward identity legislation (PL 101-644) in the arts vary. Some artists oppose it on the basis of freedom of expression. AH's statement is representative of this opinion:

> M: What are your feelings about PL 101-644?

> AH: The arts and crafts law? Oh, I think you should be allowed to do anything you want. I don't know of many freedoms left, and to have somebody tell you what you can and cannot do, I think it's detrimental, certainly, to the artist, but also to the world.

Still others oppose it as a manifestation of colonial rule. Leonard Peltier is often quoted in support of this position:

> This is not our way. We never determined who our people were through numbers and lists. These are the rules of our colonizers, imposed for the benefit of our colonizers at our expense. They are meant to divide and weaken us. I will not comply with them. (Peltier in Churchill 1992:72)

Clearly, the debate over PL 101-644 has splintered the Native American art community (see chapter 2). It has also shifted attention away from acts of racism to the definition of race, and in this sense it has served the interests of the state. Because the market for Native American art is so lucrative, and because PL 101-644 limits access to that market, passage of the law has eroded some artists' convictions against the legislation of identity. EO was raised in San Francisco, son of an Anglo mother and Santa Clara father. He graduated from a prestigious Ivy League college before attending the IAIA, and speaks eloquently about the limitations imposed on Native American artists by primitivist consumers. Ethnic authenticity should not be a requirement for tribal artists, but because it is, and because he is enrolled, EO supports PL 101-644.

M: How do you feel about PL 101-644?
EO: What?
M: The Indian Arts and Crafts Act.
EO: I think it's right. . . . I do think there is a necessity to establish criteria for selling work as Native. The idea that you should protect this commodity, I believe in that. . . . Because the market is in search of authenticity, because the market associates quantum of blood with authenticity, because authenticity equates to money, because it's a buyer's market, because my kids are on tribal roll. For all those reasons, it has to be there. Why shouldn't it be there?
M: Some artists are against it, they feel it's buying into the U.S. government's colonialist system.
EO: Yeah, that's everybody without a C.I.B. [Certificate of Indian Blood].
M: Don't you think it's odd that the federal government regulates Indian art, but not any other kind of art?
EO: No. It makes absolute sense. Because there's a federal relationship between the government and the Indians. It's land-based, there's gaming now, revenues, every aspect of our lives is related to the federal government—our health system, our scholarships, our education—do you think art wouldn't be? As much money is generated out of here [Santa Fe], with Native art, do you think that wouldn't be?

▪

With all the political and historical implications of being Native American and participating in the Native American art market, it is not surprising that some artists choose to incorporate social statements into their work. This practice is seen throughout the world where art objects or material culture have been deemed safe vehicles for the expression of resistance.[11] In the extreme view, all contemporary indigenous art is political, a declaration of survival and sovereignty. Australian Aboriginal art is often presented in this light: "All Aboriginal art is, in its essence, political. It is a statement about ownership of land and culture" (Institute of American Indian Arts 1992:n.p., see also Isaacs 1992). Among the Native American artists I interviewed, however, the integration of political or social commentary into artwork was viewed as more of a personal choice.

Artists who choose to make political statements with their work address a wide range of issues (see chapter 7). Environmental concerns inspire Lawrence Paul, a Vancouver-based artist of Coast Salish and Okanagan heritage who is better known by his tribal name of Yuxweluptun. This artist is unique among his Northwest Coast contemporaries both for his political focus and his creative appropriation of surrealism. As art historian Charlotte Townsend-Gault wrote, Yuxweluptun has developed his own "hybrid vocabulary" with which to "make an excoriating critique of systemic racism" (1998:644). Using his tribe's conventional formlines and ovoids, Yuxweluptun paints sickly, Dali-esque images of clear-cut forests, "weeping" landscapes, demonic missionaries, and shattered reservation alcoholics (see the images in Townsend-Gault 1995a). In explanation, the artist writes: "Land claims have always concerned me: fishing rights, hunting rights, water rights, inherent rights. My home, my native land. Land is power, power is land. This is what I try to paint" (Yuxweluptun 1995:1).

Navajo painter Abeyta is among those artists who choose—for the moment, at least—not to combine art with activism. In our interview, he expressed resentment toward what he perceived as a public expectation for contemporary Indian artists to make political art:

I think people say, "Indian art should make a statement, it should say that we as people are oppressed." And it's like, Jesus Christ,

you know, we have nothing to say.... There are indigenous tribes in this world that are struggling just for their own survival to live. People that are being subjected to genocide. Kids in Guatemala that are watching their parents get killed. Now, they have a statement. Now they have something to really speak about. Native Americans, yes, we have that, but for right now, I really feel that anyone with a really extreme political confrontation really needs to deal with those specific politics, or shut up. I mean, they really need to immerse themselves in what is involved in actual change. It doesn't do any good to present people with information if you don't have any kind of antidote for it. It's nice to be kind of morose, and say, well, look at the injustices done, look what they did at Wounded Knee, look what they did here, look at how Native Americans are treated when they go into restaurants in South Dakota, that's a shame. Let's work to politically change it, because that's what's really going to benefit our children. Presenting it to people [as art], people don't really act on it or really care.

It is not that Abeyta disagrees with the viewpoints of political artists. On the contrary, he supports them, having experienced the same kind of racism and discrimination as others in his position. But he values his freedom of expression, his ability to create work that is primarily aesthetic, that is about color, texture, and form.

Navajo painter Emmi Whitehorse concurs. Whitehorse was born and raised in a small town on the Navajo reservation. She attended a government boarding school for Navajo girls, then enrolled in the University of New Mexico, where she received a BA in painting and an MA in printmaking. Over the course of her career, Whitehorse has experienced poverty and racism and has associated with outspoken political artists, but her own work has remained remarkably neutral. When other Native American painters educated at Western universities and arts institutions were drawn to the gritty, confrontational styles of civil-rights era American artists, Whitehorse kept her distance (see fig. 6.1). At one point during our interview, I asked Whitehorse if she had ever considered incorporating text or political images into her work.

W: I see a lot of atrocities at home, and sometimes I want to show that to the world. But it's something that I think you would have to devote your life to, that's the way I see it. It would just totally consume me. I would be too busy reading up on issues, you know, because I would want to get my facts straight before I do something like that. So I would really probably end up almost being a scholar, first, and then trying to paint with that. I don't think it would work for me. I see it as a totally different profession. I don't know why, but I see it that way.

M: Like being an activist?

W: Yeah, I see it being more of an activist. And that would totally ... I don't think I would paint as much if I did that; it would deprive me of being in the studio. And so I choose not to deal with that, although I'm always asked to be involved in things like that, in political things. But I stay apolitical as much as possible.

M: Because it would sap your energy?

W: Yes, yes it would.

MUSEUMS ARE IMPORTANT players in the Native American art world, as they are in other art worlds. As the homes of model collections, museums are the purveyors of value and status. As collectors, they are players in the market, especially at the auction houses, where fine historic material changes hands. For a long time, museums were considered "terminal" actors in the market, the last stop on an important object's journey through time and space. Today, with repatriation legislation in effect, museums are sometimes more of a turn-around point, a space accessible to tribes seeking the use or return of their material legacy.

As collectors with resources and longevity far greater than any individual, museums are sources of power and authority. Museums play a large role in determining what is traditional or authentic, for producers as well as consumers. By displaying only the "most aesthetically suc-cessful objects" (Rushing 1995:12), museums establish a hierarchy of value against which individuals can measure their collections. Museums also alert consumers to newly desirable objects. An exhibit of one artist's work or historic material from a particular region can impact the market for that object category by increasing demand and raising prices. For individual collectors, the museum visit can become a kind of window shopping that is consummated in the museum store, a fact some Native American people find detestable because it promotes setting a value on culture (Hilden, Huhndorf, and Kalafatic 1995).

The authority of the museum is so great that few have dared to quarrel with it, at least until recent years, when museums joined their academic siblings in the post-Vietnam War politicization of scholarship. In the critical analysis that emerged, the foundations of the museum's authority—all that had been taken for granted about the acquisition, exhibition, and interpretation of objects—were thrown open to question. As the possessors of the victor's spoils, museums with holdings of Native American material culture came under particularly intense scrutiny.[1]

Much of the current literature on museums engages this critique, a sort of *ex post facto* deconstruction of the presumably imperialist intents of collection and exhibition practices. Despite the fact that colonialism has been replaced by the international art market as the "point of contact" under which objects enter museums (Vogel and Roberts 1994:77), the violence associated with colonization has not been forgotten. In fact, it is recalled and represented anew, especially as the citizens of formerly colonized nations enter the stream of museum discourse as curators and commentators. In what some have dubbed the "new museology," criticism of the museum and its practices is actually integrated into exhibits and publications.[2] According to curator Mary Nooter Roberts, "epistemological frameworks have changed so significantly in the last few decades that the notion of preserving knowledge in the positivist sense is no longer considered viable" (in Vogel and Roberts 1994:34). Curators have moved from modernist/authoritative to postmodernist/interrogative presentations of culture, and, as a result, the museum's position of authority has begun to erode.

Or has it? A number of recent exhibits have emphasized experimentation in labeling and representational techniques, as well as collaboration between Native and non-Native American consultants. In addition, tribes finally have the resources to mount their own exhibits, in which tribal historians can tell their own stories. As reports are filed from the field, however, it is clear that the audience is ambivalent about the new approach. James Clifford is one of the few critics who has expressed consistent enthusiasm, especially after his visit to two new tribal museums in Cape Mudge Village and Alert Bay, British Columbia (Clifford 1991). Others are less optimistic, especially in the wake of the Smithsonian's new National Museum of the American Indian (NMAI), which opened in October 1994 in New York City. J. Edson Way expressed a fear shared by many people when he concluded that the "discourse between indigenous and Western peoples in the gallery of the museum remains more potential than reality" (1993:110).

In this chapter, I investigate the rewards and the dilemmas new museology presents for the museum, its public, and Native American communities.

■

What is it to have a real encounter with the object? Most of these objects are radically dislocated: you're not going to encounter them in the way they were made, or in the way the people who made them encountered them—you can't even think of them that way. What's evolved over time is a certain standardized way of encountering the object.

> —*Arthur Danto, philosopher and art critic*
> *(Vogel and Roberts 1994:37)*

Most tribal people come to Indian museums carrying generations of memories. Ishi walks with us, his haunted black eyes scanning the words mounted on the walls, explaining objects in cases. We hear his voice from his museum captivity. . . . A bleak history overwhelms.

> —*Patricia Hilden, Shari Huhndorf, and*
> *Carol Kalafatic, authors of "Fry Bread and*
> *Wild West Shows: The 'New' National*
> *Museum of the American Indian" (1995:7)*

We see history where many would like to see only timeless beauty; and we see beauty where some would like us to see only injustice.

> —*Richard White, Professor of History at the*
> *University of Washington (1997:34)*

The ways in which museum visitors encounter Native American objects are shaped as much by the collective imagination of Indians and Western notions of value as by the nature of the encounter itself. Visitors enter the modern museum with certain needs and expectations: museums are expected to be simultaneously entertaining and educational, aesthetically pleasing and authoritative. Visitors need museums to validate their own experiences, to fill in the gaps in their knowledge of the world, and demonstrate the proper ways of appreciating and understanding objects and events. In the museum gallery, the visitor's needs and expectations enter into a dialogue with the curatorial voice. Unfortunately, this dialogue is usually brief.[3] The information most likely to be communicated during a short visit is that which relates, in some way, to the visitor's own (previous) experience (Graburn 1977:11–12). This is what dooms many innovative exhibits to failure, or at the very least, misinterpretation.

Anthropologist Nelson Graburn artfully described the museum visitor's experience in terms of "mythic" and "scientific" thought, a distinction originally elaborated by Claude Lévi-Strauss in *La Pensée Sauvage*. In Graburn's interpretation, scientists work "from basic principles, building up pure models and creating predictable events" (Graburn 1977:11). Ordinary folk, museum visitors included, engage in "mythic" thought, which comprehends new things on the basis of personal experience.[4] Like the *bricoleur*, who "makes new things out of the parts of the old," the museum visitor "builds new structures of understanding out of the debris of past events which [he] has experienced"

(Graburn 1977:11). The ideas with which the visitor exits the museum are the "product of a fusion of the debris of previous events and the new event of the museum experience itself" (Graburn 1977:12). Given that prior museum experiences can frequently be counted among these "previous events," the educational impact of a particular museum visit—and thus the efficacy of the new museology—is difficult to measure.

Ideally, the new museology demands a total overhaul of museum theory and practice. The primary goal is to open up space—discursive space as well as physical space—for indigenous objects to become speaking subjects who voice their own ideas and contribute to (or even seize control of) their own representations.[5] This move was instigated in part by Native American communities, who found new power in the wake of the civil-rights movement, and by select Native and non-Native American scholars, who, in exposing the imperialist roots of the anthropological project, necessarily questioned the nature of museum representations and the historical processes of acquisition. Federal repatriation legislation passed in 1990 reinforced Native American authority in the museum setting by laying down new rules for the ownership and display of tribal objects.

Museums reacted to the moral-political mandate to change in different ways and at different speeds. In retrospect, it is clear that two distinct projects emerged (and are still being carried out): historical revision, in which the actions and motivations of turn-of-the-century collectors are critiqued from the politicized vantage point of the present; and reformulation of present practices to ensure greater communication between Native and non-Native American communities. These two projects are theoretically distinct but practically linked, as Native American participation in the museum's present and future shapes the museum's understanding of its own past.

In the revision of museum history, turn-of-the-century actors are not criticized personally but rehistoricized as the intellectual products of their times. While it is widely acknowledged that museums contributed to the colonial climate that encouraged the systematic removal of objects from Indian communities, the individual collectors, anthropologists, and curators involved tend to be viewed not as willful collaborators in the colonial project but as dedicated, although unfortunately interpellated, scientists of culture. This works to indemnify the museum but fails to address the more important issue of state-sponsored violence. An example of this strategy is *Objects of Myth and Memory: American Indian Art at the Brooklyn Museum*, a comprehensive catalog of Stewart Culin's early-twentieth-century collecting activities. In it, museum curators rationalize

Culin's disinterest in living Indian people as a natural corollary to contemporary belief in the "homogeneity of Indian cultures through time and space" and the imminent doom of Indian tribes (Fane 1991:24). To be fair, the catalog's authors do raise key questions about the long-term impact of museum collecting. As reviewer Deborah Dozier paraphrased it, "Was Culin a rescuer of cultural materials? . . . Or was he a promoter of cultural depatriation, a predator scavenging from people forced away from economic independence on a cash economy?" (1992:241) But in the text these questions remained unanswered.

The collecting activities of George Gustav Heye are explored in some of the Smithsonian Institution's newer exhibits and publications (e.g., Hill and Hill 1994). Like Culin, Heye is represented as a product of his time, obsessive in his habits perhaps (Hill and Hill 1994:19), but, nevertheless, providing a valuable service to humanity. This official interpretation stands at odds with the unofficial view of Heye as a ruthless and greedy man who bought shirts off the backs of old men and stole sacred goods from burial scaffolds. "To me," reflected Crow filmmaker and Heye expert Dean Curtis Bear Claw, "in order to understand this whole collection you have to go back to 1920 and then you have to go back to 1884 . . . and then you have to go back to 1492" (in Hilden, Huhndorf, and Kalafatic

1995:26–27). In this same as-yet unpublished critique of the National Museum of the American Indian, Patricia Penn Hilden, Shari Huhndorf, and Carol Kalafatic, the Native American women co-authors, refer to Heye's collection (now in the NMAI) as a "slaughter of culture" (15). Comments such as these are absent from the museum's own exhibits and publications, despite the fact that the museum was envisioned as "an attempt to redress a long history of unbalanced and ethnocentric presentations of American Indian history and culture" (13).[6]

That a national museum would censor dissident (or unpatriotic) voices is not surprising.[7] Museums play an important role in building and maintaining the narratives of nationhood, narratives from which violence is usually excluded. This is the main difficulty with the new museology's collaborative method: how to incorporate dissident voices into the museum's expository narrative. Whereas the old museum aimed for a seamless, authoritative text, the new museum demands a text flexible enough to represent a "discursive space riddled with . . . contradictions and diverging political agendas" (Masco 1996:837). It is not enough to merely make room for Native American speakers, as so many contemporary museums have done, and done well.[8] Room must be made for Native American voices that tell the "raw truths of the Indian past out of which these objects have been seized" (Hilden, Huhndorf, and Kalafatic 1995:44).

From a theoretical viewpoint situated some distance away from the practical problems of museum management, the solution to this problem seems simple: more Native American input. James Clifford is consistently impressed by the potential of tribal contributions to reframe museum practice, in both tribal and nontribal venues (see Clifford 1988:189–251, 1989, and 1991). In 1989, Clifford served as a consultant to the Portland Art Museum's reinstallation of its Northwest Coast collection. During the initial stages of the project, Tlingit elders were invited to the museum to participate in a planning meeting. Clifford and the other museum representatives expected the elders to talk about the objects. As it turned out, the elders had a different agenda, one in which the objects inspired a "very complicated, deeply moving and sometimes lighthearted set of conversations and performances" (Clifford 1989:152). As the meeting progressed, mythic tales about salmon and a terrible octopus turned into real stories about state and federal agencies "regulating the traditional rights of Tlingits to take salmon according to their traditional protocols" (Clifford 1989:153). In other instances,

specific figures turned into the Forest Service or other governmental bodies, who were taking land away from Tlingits or restricting their use of traditional territories. So what started out as traditional stories suggested by these traditional objects ended up having very precise political meanings in terms of current struggles. (Clifford 1989:153)

The ingenuity of Native American elders in maneuvering objects to speak about the political present as well as the cultural past is impressive, but it is important to remember that this situation occurred in a meeting. The real predicament was how to communicate the agenda of the elders within the context of the museum exhibit.

Clifford suggested that the answer might be found in representing the "discrepancy between object and context prominently in exhibits" (1989:153). By "opening up, and contesting, communications around the object," power could be "decentered" long enough and in such a way as to allow for a more accurate and dialogic representation of history and culture (ibid.).

In theory, this sounds simple, but in practice it presents a serious challenge to museums, who must work within the limits of their collections, their budgets, and the political tolerances of their private and public patrons. The strategy employed by the Museum of Natural History in its 1991 exhibit "Chiefly Feasts: The

Enduring Kwakiutl Potlatch" was to divide representational authority between (primarily non-Native American) museum curators, who wrote the historical narrative, and Native American experts, who took responsibility for the section on contemporary potlatch practice. As a result, the exhibit took on the tone of an "intellectual contest" (Masco 1996:838), that presented two conflicting claims. The first "valorize[d] the contribution anthropology has made to preserving and interpreting Northwest Coast cultures." The second "place[d] that same anthropological tradition within the field of colonial practices" (Masco 1996:840). While Native American expertise was employed specifically for the contemporary section, Native American participation did influence the display of historic objects. In one instance, tribal consultants requested the omission of a controversial carving (Berlo and Phillips 1992:30). Native American experts also aided in the interpretation of historic objects, enabling curator Aldona Jonaitis to identify a disparate group of masks as belonging to a single dance cycle (Berlo and Phillips 1992:30). Because the rhetorical discrepancy between Native American and non-Native American curatorial voices remained unresolved, however, anthropologist Joseph Masco concluded that the museum's attempt to "reinvent ethnographic authority . . . remains stalled and incomplete" (1996:848).

One of the most elaborate attempts at multivocality to date was "Creation's Journey," one of the NMAI's three inaugural exhibits. In it, select "masterworks" of Native American art were displayed with multiple explanatory texts. These texts were segregated into the authorial categories of "anthropologist," "art historian," and "Native." Each category had a distinct voice: anthropological labels stressed the utilitarian value of objects; art-historical labels emphasized the aesthetic dimensions; and Native labels contextualized objects within specific cultural histories. Because the statements made in each voice were drawn from disparate sources, however, the voices were not consistent throughout the exhibit. This had the effect of undermining the distinctions between categories. What does it mean when a Native American voice mentions utility, or an anthropological voice praises the beauty of an object? Some statements were decontextualized to an extent that rendered them incomprehensible, such as the translated fragment of poem that served as the Native label for an Alaskan kayak.

As a curatorial experiment of monumental scale, the NMAI received more publicity in the national media than any other Native American museum in recent history. For several years before it opened, the museum placed advertisements in prominent publications, such as the *New York Times* and the *New Yorker*, where it claimed the "world's most extensive collection of American Indian artifacts." The museum also claimed representational authority: "When the National Museum of the American Indian opens its doors, it will open your eyes to the true heritage of Native American people." A massive membership campaign accompanied the advertisements, necessary because federal funding was contingent on a 50 percent match from private donors.

The NMAI promised unprecedented innovations in exhibit ideology and technology. As the copy in one particularly seductive advertisement read, "Any museum can invite you to look. A great one changes the way you see." According to the membership-campaign literature, this would be accomplished by putting Native Americans in charge of development. Museum director Richard West, a Southern Cheyenne lawyer whose father was a well-known artist, promised to provide a "forum" for tribal people to tell their own stories in their own words: "At last, we will see American Indians as they see themselves. Without paternalism, condescension, or racism."

Media coverage and museum publicity raised great expectations in the Native American community, as well as the museum-going public. West traveled to conferences across the country, where he outlined the museum's lofty goals, including a "virtual museum" accessible to Native American communities (Dubin 1995). Meanwhile, the actual negotiations involved in establishing the museum—from the squabble over who would get Heye's immense collection (Carpenter 1991) to the appointment of new (and primarily Native American) trustees to the actual development of exhibits (Arieff 1995)—were shrouded in secrecy.

The museum's much-feted opening on October 30, 1994, generated intense media attention but ultimately proved to be anticlimactic. Reviews were mixed, noting the beauty of the objects displayed but criticizing the "confusion" of the exhibit areas. The *New York Times* called the museum's initial effort "faltering and exploratory" (Cotter 1994:C1). The beautiful objects on display were "sabotaged," the reporter wrote, "by an overproduced installation and by a curatorial philosophy that too often favors political grandstanding and feel-good sentiment over discretion and scholarship" (ibid.). The *Wall Street Journal* objected to the lack of dates for objects throughout the exhibits. "Having decided that ethnology, anthropology, history—and even chronology—get in the way of appreciating Native Americans and their artworks for their essential qualities, the show's organizers have dispensed with such distinctions altogether" (Gamerman 1992). The *Economist* applauded the attempt to put Indians in control, but said the "video commentary tends to be a babble" (1995:81).

The NMAI's inaugural exhibits were ambitious and innovative, in tune with the sensitive

5.1.
"This Path We Travel," one
of three inaugural exhibits
at the National Museum
of the American Indian in
New York City in 1994.
Photograph by
Katherine Fogden

political environment as well as the challenging postmodern aesthetic (see fig. 5.1). However, they did not take into account the needs and expectations of the museum-going public, which still sought an authoritative experience, especially in relation to Native American objects, which are so intimately associated with history and tradition. It is at this point—the point of contact between the museum and its public—that the new museology is most likely to break down. As the published reviews of the NMAI's inaugural exhibits indicate, accessibility to the viewing public is an issue that deserves more attention. If an exhibit is a "mélange of symbolic statements that are all but indecipherable" (*Economist* 1995:81), what gets communicated to the average museum visitor during those few seconds of dialogue?

Opening day was a Sunday, and on this day alone several hundred visitors took the time to write in the comment book, or fill out a one-page survey form provided at the museum exit. Reactions to the exhibits varied widely. Many visitors echoed the criticisms of professional reviewers, but some revealed a more personal experience. A few of the comments were unconditionally positive: "This is fabulous," wrote a man from New York City. "I was moved deeply," wrote a sixty-year-old artist. Another man who was "moved to tears" contemplated the reason: "white man guilt?" A fifteen-year-old student wrote "Thanks. As a student you don't get a grasp on the Native American culture. This helped me tremendously." An Ohio teacher wrote, "Thank you for opening the world to the truth."

Some people couched their praise in criticism: "It's about time the Smithsonian established a Native American museum," wrote a forty-three-year-old man from Seattle. "It's about time that Native views predominate," wrote a teacher from New York City. People who had been frequent visitors to the collection's former home, the Museum of the American Indian at Broadway and 155th Street (see fig. 5.2), expressed dismay at the new setup. One such man called the new museum "superficial." The original museum, he wrote, "was a *real* Indian museum." One of the longest and most critical comments was written by a self-described long-time friend of the original museum:

> This is far and away the most spectacular waste of time, money, and intellect I have seen in years, maybe ever. It is expensive decor with a glaze, not even a burned-in patina, of research.... I cannot believe that the Smithsonian has transformed that magical (albeit rundown) museum into this illogical, high-tech miasma.

The only improvement as far as these Heye-

5.2. Displays on the first floor of the original Museum of the American Indian, circa 1925. Photograph courtesy of the National Museum of the American Indian, Smithsonian Institution

collection regulars were concerned was the new museum's location: "At least [it] is in a much better neighborhood than the previous museum," wrote a thirty-two-year-old computer engineer from Brooklyn.

Many visitors criticized the poor organization of the exhibits. "Organization seems confused," wrote a fifty-one-year-old psychologist. "The presentation was horrendous—very cramped, chaotic media blitz, no sense of scale, not enough space, information incomplete," wrote an artist from Chicago. One visitor said she was "looking for a theme, like pottery from various cultures." Another New York City psychologist wanted to see "more information or tags identifying individual pieces, especially the material pieces are made of." A twenty-eight-year-old museum curator was "concerned about the lack of historical documentation." Many people commented on the lack of chronological markers: "Dating eras would be helpful." A translator complained that the objects were "not presented within the context of a historical overview, or one that differentiates between tribes, locations, [or] time periods. While this may represent the latest in museology, I find it detracts from the interest and educational potential of the show."

Some of the same visitors who saw the exhibits as disorganized also resented what they perceived to be an "overly political" tone. "[I]t seems to be heavy-handed politically," wrote

the fifty-one-year-old psychologist. A retired executive called the museum a "sterile hodge podge of political correctness." A fifty-one-year-old farmer from Sioux City, South Dakota, praised the "wide variety of artifacts," but thought the "wording [was] *too* politically correct!!"

Other visitors demanded more attention to contemporary Native American concerns. One twenty-four-year-old teacher questioned the display of a Ghost Dance shirt in the "All Roads Are Good" exhibit. "They seem to be personal, sacred objects. Should they be on view?" A thirty-one-year-old social worker wrote that the museum "presents Native Americans as an extinct people with leftover beautiful trinkets," and asked the museum to "please incorporate more of existing culture."

Ironically, the mingling of commodity and aesthetic values that was critiqued by Hilden and her co-authors was a significant point of connection for museum visitors. Because many visitors—especially collectors—identify with the notion of art-as-commodity, they feel comfortable in what some critics have called the "marketplace ambiance" of the museum. The identification of museum objects as commodities is also an important component of the museum's relationship to its patrons. Because museums deal in valuable commodities, and because state support of museums has been drastically reduced in recent years, museums are more reliant than ever on patrons to support the purchase of new objects and secure the donation of important collections. Museums moralize the consumerism of collectors by associating it with the lofty ideals of education and the preservation of heritage. In return for their contributions, donors gain cultural capital.

Museums ensure the loyalty of patrons by organizing special-interest clubs in which elite members pay an additional fee to support their collecting area. At the Southwest Museum in Los Angeles, the Collectors' Club hosts lectures, workshops, and receptions for artists. The club's annual auction raises thousands of dollars for the museum. In return for their support, club members receive recognition in the museum newsletter and special discounts in the museum shop. In Santa Fe, the Museum of Indian Arts and Culture recently organized a club called Friends of Indian Art, which sponsors social events and raises funds for new acquisitions. For the $100 it costs to join the club for a year, members get invited to elegant cocktail parties at upscale galleries, where they can mingle with their favorite contemporary Indian artists (see chapter 4). They also have the satisfaction of exercising some power in the museum's decision-making process, as they approve the purchase of objects funded by their donations.

Within the museum itself, the notion of art-as-commodity is reinforced by the strategic placement of gift shops near exits or restrooms.

The NMAI has not one but two strategically positioned gift shops. The first-floor shop, which visitors pass on their way out of the museum, caters to collectors, displaying expensive rugs, pottery, and jewelry in a manner reminiscent of the museum exhibits. The basement store, across the hall from the restrooms, stocks educational supplies and children's books and toys. Several visitors praised the first-floor shop on their comment forms: "Loved the shop, and spent a good hour just there." One person was dismayed at the selection of toys in the basement shop: "If you want to teach respect, why are you selling that crap in the museum shop? Get rid of the fake tomahawks, teepees, bows and arrows, it is degrading."

Hilden and her co-authors were enraged by what they saw as a focus on commodity values throughout the museum. Visitors "see commodity values everywhere" (1995:39) in this "boutique of valuable Indian artifacts" (1995:31) that verges on a " 'fine arts' shopping mall" (1995:41). They admit that the problem is not limited to the NMAI. It is a symptom of a larger phenomenon in which sites of study and sites of consumption are formally converging, as they are rapidly on the World Wide Web. But according to Hilden and her co-authors, it is especially problematic in Native American museums, where the focus on commodity values serves the state by displacing the Native American creators, stifling their voices, and erasing their complex and violent histories. In this way the NMAI's marketplace ambiance is tied to the aforementioned censorship of dissident voices: both are manifestations of a strategy to keep the dominant society in control of Native American bodies and representations.

Without denying the validity of these observations, it is important to recognize that even the most idealistic modern museum must function within the capitalist economy. Regardless of their violent histories, Native American objects are valuable commodities, even in tribal museums located on the decommoditized territory of tribal lands. The U'mista Cultural Society in Alert Bay, British Columbia, learned this the hard way in the summer of 1995, when a valuable frontlet was stolen before the museum had purchased adequate insurance.

▪

Regardless of any flaws in its conception, the NMAI makes a significant move toward "opening up and contesting communications around the object" (Clifford 1989:153). It is a move other large metropolitan museums—rendered inert by nostalgia and disciplinary precedents—have not even been able to contemplate. In New York City, for example, other permanent exhibits of Native American art remain lodged in the antiquated frameworks of Boasian ethnology or natural history. At the Museum of Natural History, display techniques date back to the early twentieth century, when material culture was mounted in glass cases, like so many insect specimens pinned to felt boards. In the famous Hall of Northwest Coast Indians, neatly typed labels separate objects into categories based on function—"ceremonial objects," "tools and utensils," "pipes and games." A nostalgic contingent vigorously opposes any change to this famous hall, claiming it as a historical landmark in museum anthropology. After all, this is the place Franz Boas brought his students to "practice" anthropological fieldwork, and these are the objects whose fantastic associations inspired Claude Lévi-Strauss (1982).

To make matters worse, Native American art is almost entirely absent from New York City's major museums of art: the Metropolitan, the Whitney, the Museum of Modern Art, and the Guggenheim. The Met's display of non-Western objects highlights African and Oceanic sculptures and masks, part of the legacy left by the Museum of Primitive Art. Two contemporary Native American artists (James Luna and Jimmie Durham) were invited to participate in the Whitney's 1993 Biennial Exhibition, a show whose multiculturalism was perhaps inspired by the Columbus quincentennial (see chapter 7). Neither MOMA nor the Guggenheim collects art made by Native Americans. The disinterest of tight mainstream art museums in contemporary Native American work has forced upon the NMAI and other exclusively Indian institutions the unsavory association of "reservation," as these are the only museum venues open to the historic continuum of Native American art.

Many small, regional museums throughout the country haven't even started to engage the new museology, if anthropologist Kathleen Dahl's findings in the states of Washington, Oregon, Idaho, and Montana are representative. Dahl spent a summer touring Pacific Northwest museums, historical societies, and cultural centers to find out how Native American history and culture were being portrayed to the public. She was particularly interested in comparing exhibits in Native and non-Native American facilities, expecting to find more accurate information in the former. To her surprise, she found that tribal facilities were just as likely to focus on romanticized images as were non-tribal museums.[9] To her dismay, Dahl found little evidence of the new museology anywhere. In both types of facilities, Dahl received the impression that "Indians no longer exist in any recognizable form, only traditional cultural characteristics are valuable, and Indians today are valued primarily for their links to the past" (1997:7). The main difference, she noted, was that tribal museums "feature[d] text in [the] first person."

Dahl's study points to another, more subtle but equally important difference between tribal and non-tribal representations of culture and history. Where non-tribal museums tend to occlude violence, most often with a pacifying rhetoric that translates the massacres of tribal people into "accidental outcomes brought about by otherwise well-intentioned people" (Dahl 1997:9), tribal facilities tend to exclude contemporary controversies, such as casino gaming. This is consistent with tribal narratives of nationhood, in which tribes see themselves as distinct traditional cultural groups descended directly from original, historic groups. Narratives of this nature foster positive feelings about ethnic identity by emphasizing physical and cultural continuity. Not coincidentally, this is the narrative required by the federal government in its program for recognizing Indian groups as tribes, which enables members to receive federal benefits (see chapter 2).

In pointing out the subjective and politically strategic nature of tribal self-representations, Dahl argues against the widely held but problematic assumption that any Native American voice is better than any non-Native American voice. Native and non-Native American scholars alike have employed this assumption with good intentions, certainly, and museums use it because it is a safe and easy solution to the contemporary crisis of authority. But shifting the responsibility into Native American hands is no guarantee of a more accurate, or more counter-hegemonic, representation. In his critical review of the NMAI, Richard White identifies the crucial problem: "Identity does not bestow knowledge" (1997:29). In reference to the NMAI, White (unwittingly) joins Hilden and other Native American critics when he concludes that "the false claims of earlier generations of scholars and curators are not necessarily corrected by replacing them with Indian voices" (1997:29).

This argument is supported by two logics. First, there is the valid concern that museums (and other institutions) may hire Indians as mere tokens of ethnic pluralism. As David W. Penney (1995) has pointed out, Native American voices can become part of a "politically-correct trope" in which different words are used to convey the same information. Second, there is the suspicion that modern Indians have been interpellated by the dominant society to such an extent that their self-representation would not differ from the "empowered group's representation of their otherness" (Dominguez 1987:136). While there are seeds of truth in this argument, too often it is used to disempower and divide. Note how Tim Giago, publisher of the largest Indian newspaper in the country, dismisses the curatorial efforts of the NMAI because there are "few—if any— American Indians working for [the museum]" (1991:n.p.). With the majority of the museum's staff listed as enrolled tribal members, what Giago means here is that there are few "real," uninterpellated Indians working for the museum. "It is . . . about time that Mr. West [the museum's director, an enrolled Southern Cheyenne] hire some genuine, traditional Indians to advise him, as it is apparent that he . . . has little knowledge about the real history of the American Indian" (1991:n.p.).

This leads us to the real problem of dissent within tribal communities. Not only are an increasing number of Native Americans joining the museum community, but Native American communities are frequently divided over the interpretation of cultural objects and historical events. Participants in the Hopi Tribal Museum Project have encountered difficulty in "arriving at a local consensus about the nature of [the Hopi] worldview, . . . and how much of it should be displayed" (Way 1993:122). Another common conflict centers around the use of funds. The treasurer of the U'mista Cultural Society in Alert Bay, British Columbia, responded to an "extremely critical" letter by writing a long article in the Society's newsletter detailing the management of money. "The people and/or organizations that are the most critical seem to have the perception that vast amounts of money flow into U'mista's coffers. This is nowhere near the truth," the treasurer wrote (Sanborn 1995:10). Other tribal museums have had to answer to charges of corruption, theft, or nepotism. Disinterest is also an issue: some tribal people dismiss the museum concept altogether, likening it to a cultural tomb.

Museums cannot escape their past. Ishi's eyes and Ishi's voice are always there, lurking in the dark passageways between curatorial intentions, visitor experiences, and political realities. But the present openness to change and to dialogue, the new sense of responsibility to Native American peoples, and the enthusiastic exchange of personnel between museum and tribal communities (e.g., the Smithsonian Institution's internship program for Native American students) bode well for a future in which museums serve Native American communities as well as Native American communities have served them.

VISIT YOUR NEIGHBORHOOD bookstore, or scan the arts section of your local newspaper, and you could get the impression that Native American artworks are either primitive objects fashioned from animal carcasses by a people long dead or adolescent pictures produced by living people mired in their spiritual past. Such objects are neither the relics of great civilizations nor the experiments of vibrant artistic communities filled with existential angst. They are the products of primitive society, or, alternatively, the products of poverty—responses to market demand that are better suited to home decorating than art criticism.

This is how Native American art gets written in most of the popular press. It is a simple and powerful vision, easily adaptable to coffee-table books and fully supported by the discourse of the imagined Indian. Unfortunately, it is a vision that stands undisturbed by the bulk of American scholarly research and writing. During the early-

twentieth-century artifactual mode of anthropology, Native American art remained inaccessible or deeply contextualized. To borrow a phrase from Gerald Vizenor, Indian objects were reduced to the mere evidence of culture. In the purview of art historians, tribal artists have received more individual attention. But as cultural Others whose aesthetic traditions are embedded in an unrecorded past, tribal artists are consistently separated from their non-Native American peers. They are withheld from the flux of time, denied their place in what anthropologist Joseph Masco eloquently terms a "shared modernity" (1996:844, see also Fabian 1983).

In this chapter, I argue for a history of Native American art that is politically informed and a criticism of contemporary Native American fine arts[1] that is historically founded. To understand the system that connects history to criticism, and the whole of art writing to the production and consumption of artworks, I turned to sociologist Howard S. Becker's *Art Worlds* (1982).[2] In this book, Becker described the social network that connects people who do different jobs (e.g., production, distribution, evaluation) in the Western art world. Because his focus was cooperation, the division of labor is understood as a practical issue. When this model is applied to the Native American art world, however, the division of labor is revealed to be overwhelmingly political. Where Becker's sociological approach eclipsed power relations in the mainstream art world, it highlighted the profoundly unequal power relations in the Native American art world, where labor tends to be divided along ethnic lines. This chapter outlines both the mechanisms of cooperation and the racialist division of labor in the context of the published writings of the Native American art world's sanctioned scribes.

■

Early contributions to Native American art history paralleled American patronage of Native American arts in the 1920s and 1930s (see Berlo 1992). During this period a significant shift in federal policy occurred, signaled by the end of land allotments and the institution of economic-recovery programs, such as the Indian Arts and Crafts Board Act of 1935. While some crafts had already found favor in the public eye as emblems of the Arts and Crafts Movement, others had been officially discouraged,

or banned outright as accessories to a barbaric lifestyle. In the Depression-era political climate, Indian products were reclaimed as part of America's heritage. At the urging of enthusiastic patrons of the arts, the government supported the revival of traditional crafts and the development of new ones as a means for tribes to achieve economic independence.

The subsequent renaissance of material culture was publicized by major museum shows, such as the "Exposition of Indian Tribal Arts" (1931) and "Indian Art of the United States" (1941), both in New York City (for more information on these exhibits, see Rushing 1995:97–120). Catalogs published in conjunction with these exhibits called for a body of literature distinct from the material-culture literature of anthropology. Ethnographies were useful references, especially where they reconstituted authentic forms, but their emphasis on utility in the tribal context was inappropriate for objects destined to be used as decorations in non-Native American homes.[3] In accord with Indian art's promotion from "artifact" to "art," consumers wanted confirmation of an object's worth outside its context of production, along with professional explanations of aesthetic continuity and change.

The first historians of Native American art faced a task of mammoth proportions: a people formerly thought to be dead, or dying, were producing arts that were believed to be connected to an ancient but unwritten history. The notion that modern, industrialized America could sustain such a people, and such a production, inspired prose filled with patriotic reveries and romantic sentiments. In his introduction to the catalog for the Exposition of 1931, Herbert J. Spinden, curator of the Department of Ethnology at the Brooklyn Museum, praised the "natural abilities" of "the Indian." He reminded readers that Indian art is part of the American heritage, and he suggested that by reclaiming this heritage Americans could recover their souls.

> We have in our Indians a reality of Arcady that is not dead, a spirit that may be transformed into a potent leaven of our own times. . . . Shall it be said that we conquered the world and lost ourselves, that we slew beauty as a vain sacrifice to unsufficing machines? (1931:8)

Held up as the ideal in a critique of modern industrialism, "the Indian" fared hardly better than before, when his lifestyle had been disparaged. Though recalled fondly, he was still primitive, singular, and stereotyped, still separate from a modernity wrought by colonialism.

The catalog for "Indian Art of the United States" retreated somewhat from the pulpit of primitivism. This exhibition, mounted at the Museum of Modern Art by Rene d'Harnon-court, manager of the Indian Arts and Crafts Board, and Frederic Douglas, curator of Indian art for the Denver Art Museum, was designed to support the new federal program for Indian artists. To this end, it included examples of contemporary work. Still, most of the catalog was reserved for historic objects, which the curators separated into geographic regions that echoed ethnographic culture areas. Following the criteria of anthropologists, adherence to tradition was identified as the key characteristic of authenticity. Because contemporary works diverged from this ideal, or perhaps because there was no established strategy for historicizing new media and forms, new work was discussed separately, in a section titled "Indian Art for Modern Living" (see chapter 2). Here the curators advocated patronage of Indian crafts not as a moral action but an economic one, practical for both producers and consumers. In places the prose approached propaganda, lauding contemporary products for their utilitarian and decorative functions within the modern American home.

The production of contemporary arts and crafts persisted after government support waned (for information on the decline of the Indian Arts and Crafts Board after World War II, see Schrader 1983:278–298). Native American art history continued to be written primarily as a survey of authentic forms, with evaluation based on adherence to tradition.[4] The interpretation of works that made use of Western media and techniques remained weak, a testimony to the popularity of the imagined Indian and a consequence of the occlusion of colonial history. Beyond allusions to a far-distant past in which all Indians were artists and all art was utilitarian, new forms remained unconnected to history and to the larger events that shaped the worlds of their creators.[5]

The 1971 publication of *Indian Painters and White Patrons* by J. J. Brody marked a critical turning point. A revised version of his dissertation in art history at the University of New Mexico, Brody's book was the first serious attempt to contextualize the artistic renaissance of the '20s and '30s within the social and political dynamics of an emerging (and imperialist) art world.

Today Brody is a preeminent scholar in the field of Native American art history, but at the time he was a relative newcomer. Brody encountered Indian art for the first time in the 1950s, while a student at the University of New Mexico in Albuquerque. As he recalled many years later in a lecture at the Oakland Museum (Brody 1997), he approached Indian art from the viewpoint of an urban person trained in Western fine arts. What intrigued him most was the apparently easy coexistence of new and old forms, and, within the medium of painting, what he perceived as the emphasis on stylistic conformity over quality. Brody couldn't understand why collectors made such a fuss over the flat paintings produced at the Santa Fe Studio School. To his eye, much of this work was "sugar candy," decorative yet unfulfilling.

Brody decided to investigate the genealogy of Native American easel painting. Was this increasingly popular form the extension of an ancient tradition, as early art historians described it, or was it new, an "invented tradition" encouraged by Euro-Americans within the patronizing dynamic of colonialism? The topic raised some eyebrows in the art history department. "Remember," Brody recalled in his lecture,

This was the late '60s. The Civil Rights movement was just ten years old. The general consensus among whites in the Southwest was that [Indian objects] were not "art," that they were made because of social circumstances. They were traditional and not creative. It was a novel idea then, to look at Native American art as a historically explicable event. (1997)

Indian Painters and White Patrons, the book that grew out of Brody's doctoral dissertation, departed from previous histories of Native American art in several ways. Most significant, perhaps, was its structure, which juxtaposed a conventional culture-area history of prehistoric "pictorial arts" with a political history of Indian-white relations. At first glance, the summary of federal Indian policy seems unrelated, or at best tangential, to the development of Indian arts. Previous art historians and anthropologists had certainly thought so, attributing change to natural rather than social or political forces. But as Brody moves through the major historical events, from the so-called Indian wars to reservations, boarding schools, the Dawes Act, and finally the New Deal, it grows clear that he is setting the stage for a crucial moment, one shaped by history more than any natural aesthetic evolution.

In the most powerful section of the book, Brody revealed the racist nature of Anglo-American participation in both the craft revival and the development of easel painting in the Southwest. Against a backdrop of severe social and economic depression in Indian country, wealthy immigrant whites easily assumed the dominant role in patronage relationships in which Indians were encouraged to paint images of their traditional activities. In virtually all of these relationships, Indian artists were "treated as social and intellectual inferiors" (Brody 1971:89). According to Brody, "[e]ven the most sensible, humanistic, and scientifically objective of the Whites seemed unable to avoid (or even recognize) attitudes that can be described only as paternalistic and racist" (1971:90). Anglo-American patrons of the arts hired Indians as stable-boys and janitors, then encouraged them to paint scenes of their traditional lives. In paintings by the patrons, Indians were likewise portrayed not as hired hands, but romantically, as traditionalists. Not surprisingly, Brody concluded that despite any continuities in form, modern Indian painting had developed in response to the needs of the dominant society. Easel paintings became the currency of social welfare, accessories to the ethnographic record (see Parsons 1962), instruments of cultural critique, and decor in non-Native American homes. Even if Native Americans later "took" painting and made it their own, as Brody noted in the last chapter, the medium's early history stood as a reminder of the intimate connection between colonial and art histories.

Reactions to *Indian Painters and White Patrons* were mixed. As Brody later recalled, painting dealers were upset because the book seemed to undermine their claim to be selling authentic Indian art.

> Traders were shocked, some never spoke to me again. They saw what I was doing as entirely subversive of their profession. [They thought of Indian art as] works produced in a primitive tradition. They couldn't see the history. (1997)

This reaction was consistent with the overwhelming disregard for colonial history in the marketplace, where any Native American object, no matter how violently or unethically obtained, was fair game for sale (and profit).

Brody's reading of the situation not only implicated traders in the colonialist system of patronage but it devalued easel paintings, stripping from them the authenticity provided by their link to the pre-contact past.

On the other hand, Brody recalled, Marxist colleagues applauded the book as a classic exposition of class struggle. In this reading, Indian artists were seen as passive participants in a system that was simultaneously racist and capitalist, and paintings were a symbol of their oppression. Then and now, Brody disavowed this interpretation, pointing out that an individual's participation in this nascent art world was voluntary. The ultimate goal of *Indian Painters and White Patrons* was not to moralize but to analyze an art form, to develop a strategy for distinguishing "good" paintings from "bad." In the long run, Brody concluded, the patronage system produced paintings that were bad, "timid" in their reluctance to confront the circumstances of their genesis and "sterile" in their blunt commercialism.

Brody's strategy of interweaving aesthetic and socio-political histories was radical, prescient of the concerns of the "new" art historians. But while no one could deny the impact of colonial history and Euro-American desire on Native American art, other art historians were slow to incorporate Brody's politically informed narrative into their own writing. They preferred the romantic and politically sanitized approach of

Dorothy Dunn's *American Indian Painting of the Southwest and Plains Areas* (1968). Dunn taught Indian students how to paint on paper, yet she insisted that "Indian painting [was] New World conceived," that it revealed

> the aboriginal concept of man's relationship with the unique American environment—the soil and the gigantic terrain, the powerful natural forces, the indigenous substances and beings. (Dunn 1968:xxvi)

Like the traders who dismissed Brody's book, Dunn viewed Native American painting as a natural outgrowth of a primitive artistic tradition and thus denied Native American artists their rightful place in a "shared" and rapidly changing modernity.

■

Meanwhile, outside of the museums and the universities, Native Americans were busy dismantling their romantic image by voicing political concerns and engaging in protests. By the late '60s it became clear that federal efforts to hasten assimilation through termination and relocation had failed. Alienated from their land and cut off from federal services, urban Indians across the country joined forces in political actions, such as the takeover of Alcatraz Island (1969–71) and the occupation of Wounded

Knee (1973). Some tribal artists responded to the tenor of the times by incorporating social and political commentaries into their work (see Wye 1988:46–47). But America's idealized vision of art as apolitical, coupled with the vision of Indian art as hailing from a primitive tradition, effectively sequestered these works from the more impassioned coverage of current events.[6]

A rather curious exception to this practice was the July-August 1972 issue of *Art in America*, a "special issue" dedicated to "The American Indian." This atypical issue addressed an eclectic group of political and historical topics, including "The Indian in the Western Movie," "The Artist-Explorers," and "Black Mesa: Progress Report on an Ecological Rape." Only two articles were about Indian art: the now-famous "23 Contemporary Indian Artists," by the Lumbee artist and curator Lloyd Oxendine, and "The Navajo Blanket," by non–Native American art historians Tony Berlant and Mary Kahlenberg.

While the latter article was unremarkable, Oxendine's piece was noteworthy in several respects: it was one of the first surveys of exclusively modernist Native American art, and it was one of the first surveys of any kind written by a tribal person. As an artist and curator, Oxendine was privy to recent developments in the Native American art world. He acknowledged the importance of the newly founded Institute of American Indian Arts (IAIA) in Santa Fe, New Mexico, a school where young artists from across the country were learning the techniques of modernism and the cultural language of pan-Indianism. He interpreted contemporary work as a response to these techniques and as a reaction to the conservatism of early-twentieth-century Indian painting. In a significant reversal of the Western tendency to position Native American artists outside the discourse of modern experience, Oxendine recognized tribal artists as participants and innovators. He described the transformation of conventional forms into protest art, contemporary expressions of the "radicalization of younger Indians in the late sixties" (Oxendine 1972:59). Indian art executed within the new political consciousness could finally be seen as part of a larger movement in response to social circumstances, the "American counter-culture."[7] This helped Native American artists gain visibility on the national scene.

As artists such as Bill Soza (Cahuilla/Apache), David Bradley (Chippewa), and Jean LaMarr (Paiute/Pit River) responded directly to the issues and events of the times, the connection between aesthetic production and social context became more difficult to ignore.[8] At the same time, it became increasingly difficult to connect contemporary to historic forms. Critics of Western art encourage viewers to understand the avant-garde in terms of its engagement with and rupture from historical precedent. In the Native American art world, however, old and new forms exist simultaneously and self-consciously. Parodies of the old share space with studied recreations and radical innovations. This simultaneous production of disparate forms was impossible to reconcile with the Western concept of aesthetic evolution.

In the absence of an established strategy for critiquing contemporary Native American artwork, writers relied (and frequently still rely) on an interpretive framework based on the Western qualitative oppositions of traditional/contemporary and art/craft. The distinction between "traditional" and "contemporary" refers to proximity to precontact media or forms. The distinction between "craft" and "art" is nominally about quality, but frequently reduces to a separation of media along the lines of traditional/contemporary. The arbitrary nature of these distinctions allows them to be reconstituted to accommodate unfamiliar works. The hierarchical nature of these distinctions is invidious, recalling the colonial separation of "artifact" from "art." The terms are especially troublesome to contemporary artists who reject racial authenticity as a measurement of quality.

Pueblo potter Nathan Youngblood was delighted to receive an invitation from the White House to participate in a 1995 exhibit of the nation's finest crafts. In his comment to a reporter, however, he made it clear that he con-sidered himself an "artist," not a "craftsperson." "In the last twenty-five years," Youngblood said, "artists have taken pottery to such a level that people are beginning to understand there is a possibility of its being fine-art quality and not just craft" (Youngblood in Patton 1995:55). Haisla/Northern Kwakiutl artist Lyle Wilson discards the distinction altogether: "These two labels are inadequate—perhaps irrelevant—in their description of the artistic process" (Wilson in Duffek 1989:n.p.).

The need for a new critical framework approached crisis level in the early '90s, when hundreds of artists reacted to America's celebration of the Columbus quincentenary with works that were simultaneously culturally grounded, politically aware, and formally avant-garde. Meanwhile, the epistemological crisis of Western art history (Belting 1987, Rees and Borzello 1988, Minor 1994) finally reached the Native American art world, where it demanded the production of texts more inclusive (e.g., Phillips 1995a), more attentive to social and political context (e.g., Berlo 1992, Rushing 1995, Townsend-Gault 1991, 1995a, 1995b), and more connected to other art worlds (e.g., Lippard 1990).

In the ideology of the "new" art history, distinctions between traditional/contemporary and art/craft can be dismissed as academic antinomies that deny tribal products the stature and complexity of Western arts. In practice, however, it is difficult to speak around them. The concept of a "Native American Fine Arts Movement," for example, has acquired currency among critics as well as artists and collectors. According to Margaret Archuleta and Rennard Strickland, who moved the phrase into popular usage in their 1991 *Shared Visions* exhibit at the Heard Museum in Phoenix, this "movement" encompasses twentieth-century painters and sculptors whose work draws on European and American conceptions of art as much as tribal traditions. The term is useful, but its definition is problematic because it "perpetuates the specious distinction between 'fine arts' and 'crafts'" that has historically segregated Native American artists (Rushing 1992b:6).

The very existence of a cohesive field of objects capable of being gathered under the rubric of Native American art is dubious. With producers hailing from more than 500 different cultural groups, any formal unity derives more from shared social and historical experiences than a precontact intertribal aesthetic.[9] The prevalence of brightly colored palettes and pictographic symbols in the work of contemporary Southwestern artists, for example, has less to do with a pan-Indian aesthetic than with the expectations of non-Indian consumers. But because criticism is expected to build on the foundation laid by art history, and because so much of Native American art history has been romantic and apolitical, critics tend to interpret

contemporary abstract works as extensions of an ancient, pan-Indian, symbol-laden aesthetic.

Artists find this humorous and sad. As one character remarks in Rennard Strickland's fictional but uncannily accurate drama,

It's kinda funny to think of white men standing over modern Indian nonrepresentational paintings, looking for tipis and buffalo and war bonnets in an abstract design, and declaring it Indian on the basis of the number of triangles that might be taken for tipis. (1986:294)

■

I want real art critics and historians to look at us, not dingbat anthros and Boy Scout hobbyists.
—*Joan Redbird, fictional Indian artist in Rennard Strickland's drama, "Tall Visitor at the Indian Gallery; or, The Future of Native American Art" (1986:305)*

Artists complain about not getting serious criticism. Well, I say, "Fine, hang your work in a public space and I'll do my job."
—*W. Jackson Rushing, critic and historian of Native American art (1997)*

In 1961, Clement Greenberg made one of his most famous proclamations on art. "In the long run," he wrote, "there are only two kinds of art:

the good and the bad." Most citations end here, reinforcing the notion that Greenberg's art criticism was both elitist and arbitrary. This may be the case, but consider his statement in context:

> This difference [between good and bad art] cuts across all other differences in art. At the same time, it makes all art one. No matter how exotic, a given body of art—as Chinese painting, African sculpture, Persian weaving—will begin to assimilate itself to the art with which we are already familiar as soon as we recognize the difference between the good and the bad in it. (1993 [1961]:117)

Regardless of the ethnocentrism in a Western art critic's method of evaluation, the inclusion of non-Western arts (if only temporarily) in the field of objects worth judging raises their status in a way that cultural relativism cannot. By comparing Chinese painting, African sculpture, and Persian weaving to "the arts with which we are already familiar," Greenberg acknowledged their quality outside of their cultural context. He moved "exotic" objects out of the officially objective field of ethnology and into the more emotional field of art criticism.

Some scholars say this is a terrible mistake, that non-Western objects need their context to stay meaningful. Others discard the whole concept of art criticism, associating its positive manifestation with patronage and its negative manifestation with censorship. It is not my intention here to assess the value of criticism or the necessity of cultural context for the interpretation of art objects.[10] Instead, it is to acknowledge that criticism influences the market and that many contemporary Native American artists feel they are denied the attention of professional critics. Artists who wish to engage with the mainstream contemporary art world, in particular, dismiss the typical coverage of their work as amateur and full of clichés characterizing the disjuncture of an Indian-in-the-white-man's-world.

"There's not a lot of serious art criticism about any particular artist within the Native American [community]," complained the Navajo painter Tony Abeyta. Critics "like the idea of the creative spirit among Native Americans," but because they don't understand the complexities of being an Indian artist, Abeyta said, they write about Indian art as a cultural phenomenon. "They say, 'Indian art is a regional, Southwestern, appease-the-White-people device....[And] Indians are still just evolving from selling trinkets and baubles under the portal, but they're doing it through galleries.'"

Ignorance coupled with primitivist preconceptions makes for a particularly patronizing brand of criticism. Navajo painter Emmi Whitehorse laughed as she recalled one writer who flew in from California to ask her about shamanism:

6.1.
"Rushing Water"
by Emmi Whitehorse
(Navajo), 1999, oil
and chalk on paper.
Photograph courtesy
of the artist

I was trying very hard to steer him in the other direction, but he kept coming back to the subject. It's something that I don't have a business in, because that's a totally different profession.... I think his impression must have been that we, as Native people, [that] there is religion and there is ritual to everything we do, every day. Not so, especially now, most people just watch t.v. all day, and there's nothing to that, there's no ceremony involved in that.

At the other end of the spectrum are those writers who interpret Whitehorse's ethereal brushless oils (see fig. 6.1) in terms of their affinity to the work of Paul Klee and other modern European primitivists. For example, a writer for *Art Guide* magazine wrote: "[T]he bright colors and fanciful shapes of many of Whitehorse's pastels suggest the whimsy of Klee or Dubuffet" (*Art Guide* 1988:21). Santa Fe critic Lis Bensley wrote that "Whitehorse's style suggests many influences: her own heritage with her petroglyph-like figures, and the effect [of] Mark Rothko and Paul Klee" (1993:n.p.). In the magazine *ArtSpace*, William Peterson claimed that "Like Klee, [Whitehorse] uses a free-associational approach of mobile fantasy, in which a fragile, searching line develops a personal pictographic vocabulary among shifting planes of color" (1990:38). Whitehorse did study the history of Western art at the University of New Mexico, and she is a

great admirer of Rothko, but she describes the sources of her imagery as highly personal, derived from life experiences that may or may not be related to her reservation upbringing or university training. Many critics have difficulty acknowledging that inspiration can come from sources that are eclectic and, sometimes, very ordinary (for example, one of Whitehorse's inspirations was the image of a bird on a Belgian beer label).

To be fair, few critics specialize in contemporary Native American art. Most of the reviews published in American newspapers and magazines are written by people with little knowledge of Native American culture, art history, or the processes by which Native American artists learn their medium and negotiate the market. As a result, reviews tend to read more like reports than critiques.

Cherokee painter Kay WalkingStick identifies the lack of "serious critical discussion of Native American art outside of its relationship to ethnographic or tribal art and artifacts" as one of the biggest problems facing contemporary Indian artists (1992:15). "Good, risky, original art is being done by Native Americans," WalkingStick writes (see fig. 6.2). "It is deserving of serious critical analysis and it takes no great leap of faith to analyze or appreciate it" (WalkingStick 1992:15).

Native American artists want criticism on a par with that of elite Western artists, not the

6.2. "Talking Leaves" (pages 11 and 12) by Kay WalkingStick (Cherokee), 1993, handmade book. Photograph courtesy of June Kelly Gallery, New York

watered-down versions reserved for children and the creators of the *art brut* collected by Jean Dubuffet. To Whitehorse, thoughtful criticism is an acknowledgment of quality. "The work has to be intriguing enough . . . [to] provoke a dialogue with a critic," she explained. In this way, even negative criticism is useful: "If [the critics] have a fine-art training, I'll respect their review." At the same time, many artists are ambivalent about criticism from non-Indians, even well-trained non-Indians, because the structure of the situation replicates the power relations of imperialism.[11] There are times, said Whitehorse, "when a critic comes in and previews a work, and he says this work stinks, because it's badly painted," and the artist won't accept this judgment:

> The artist will say, "That's easy for [the critic] to say that, because he's a white person. He has no business telling me how to paint." It's like being Native American gives him an excuse to do bad art and get away with it.

Criticism from Native American peers is not always an improvement. Negative comments can be interpreted as an attack on the unity of the Native American art community or dismissed as jealousy. As one Hopi painter explained, the Native American art community is suffused with an "us versus them" attitude that falls out along the racial division of labor. Tribal people who "cross over" into the careers of critic, historian, museum curator, or gallery owner are viewed with some degree of suspicion.

■

Greenberg's call for a pluralistic appreciation of aesthetic quality is valiant, but nowhere does he suggest a strategy for determining the good and the bad in the arts of the "other." This is not surprising, given the inscrutability of his own methods for evaluating Western art. But the notion of connoisseurship, especially white male connoisseurship, is anathema to proponents of feminist and ethnic arts. Lucy R. Lippard dismissed Greenberg's concept of transcendent quality as a masked form of ethnocentrism that functions to exclude rather than include. "The notion of Quality," wrote Lippard, "has been the most effective bludgeon on the side of homogeneity in the modernist and postmodernist periods" (1990:7). Yet, Lippard herself recognizes quality, hailing it as the inspiration for her book on multicultural art, *Mixed Blessings: New Art in a Multicultural America*: "[T]his book was written because artists and writers of color are making some of the most substantial art being made today" (1990:10). And like other well-known critics, her method of measuring quality remains mysterious. This leaves us with an essential dilemma: If art can be critiqued, and indeed should be critiqued, how should the arts of people both different and unfamiliar be approached?

In the Western art world, criticism and history go hand-in-hand. History provides criticism with a structuring framework, a continuous field of objects in which—or against which—new works can be situated. Conversely, criticism revives art history with a sense of occasion. With the passage of time, of course, the art of criticism becomes the art of history, a rationalized element of the aesthetic continuum.

What keeps Western art history distinct from other art histories, and allows it to progress in a linear fashion, is the persistence of a socially or culturally bounded group of producers. Western artists do "borrow" elements from the aesthetic repertoires of other cultures, but this is usually interpreted not as ethnic mutiny but as a temporary and incidental cross-fertilization inspired by specific historic conditions. When Adolph Gottlieb incorporated Native American images into his *Pictographs* series, for example, he was responding to what has frequently been described as an impasse in American painting.

> Equally dissatisfied with the often pious sentiments of regionalism, the aggressive yet uninspiring mode of American social realism, and the mechanistic aspects of geometric abstraction, . . . Gottlieb felt compelled to find his own voice, one

more in tune with the tumultuous events at the outbreak of World War II. (Kotik 1994:59)

Gottlieb was participating in the art history of his own community, which in a time of social and political crisis sought solace in the wisdom of a primal unconscious, as represented by the arts of ancient and "primitive" societies (for more information on Gottlieb's interest in Native American art, see Rushing 1995:161–68).

This kind of aesthetic freedom has not been available to non-Western artists. Those who claim membership in formerly "primitive" cultures, in particular, are expected to perpetuate their own historical forms. Indian people are generally viewed as more connected to the past—often an imagined past—than to the present. Because they are not seen as equal participants in a shared modernity, their appropriations of non-Native American forms and styles are frequently viewed as mimicry rather than intelligent responses to larger human conditions.

Conversely, the revival of tribal forms is often seen as a direct continuation of ancient traditions rather than an appropriation of symbols in promotion of sovereignty or a personal aesthetic choice. When Native Californian artists Harry Fonseca (see fig. 6.3) and Frank LaPena found inspiration in the prehistoric rock art of North America, for example, they were maintaining a "spiritual connection"

6.3.
"Stone Poem
#43" by
Harry Fonseca
(Maidu), 1989,
mixed media
on unstretched
canvas.
Photograph
courtesy of
the artist

(Archuleta 1988:21) and "bridging the chasms of time and history" (Bernstein 1988:n.p.). But the artists' own discourse tends to disturb the neat separation of Native American and Western art histories. LaPena, a Wintu painter and printmaker who teaches art at California State University-Sacramento, said he "looks at Chumash rock art through the eyes of an Abstract Expressionist" (LaPena 1997). With these words, LaPena confounds the critic who would connect his work to some prehistoric tradition.

■

Given the persistent prioritization of authenticity over quality, it is not surprising that there is very little criticism—in the sense of this-is-good, this-is-bad—of Native American art. In the absence of an accepted strategy for evaluation, the overwhelming majority of writing is concerned not with judgment but with the maintenance and reconciliation of difference. Like the process of collecting, the process of writing has been framed by the tension between sameness and otherness, haunted by the conflicting desires to reconcile difference and to exoticize. This is manifested in the rhetorical moves that establish alterity then reduce it by the invocation of familiar stereotypes.

A brief review of "The Submuloc Show" in the *Washington Post* typifies this maneuver. This 1992 show was one of several traveling exhibitions prompted by the 500th anniversary of Columbus's arrival in America. Sponsored and curated by Atlatl, a national Native American artists' association, the show included politically informed works by tribal artists who had been working in modernist styles for years. The writer from the *Post*, however, saw primitives wielding paintbrushes: "With newspaper texts and videos appearing beside totems and beads, it is clear that Indian art is an actively evolving tradition." Alterity established, the writer takes refuge in the ecological-Indian stereotype: "[T]hanks to native beliefs in the sacredness of the Earth, [the show] provides a breath of fresh air in the midst of this country's environmental muddlings" (McCoy 1992:n.p.).

In another example, a 1989 interview with Apache sculptor Bob Haozous is prefaced by musings that recall the imagined Indians of Pearce and Berkhofer.

When Haozous speaks about the natural, he means an Indian cultural relationship to nature, uncontaminated by Western civilization. Similarly, Haozous' discussion of the individual must be understood as deeply embedded within a communal society. . . . In sharp contrast to the Romantic vision of the individual, . . . the contemporary Indian artist shapes his relationship to the community from the tradition of the shaman or warrior who is

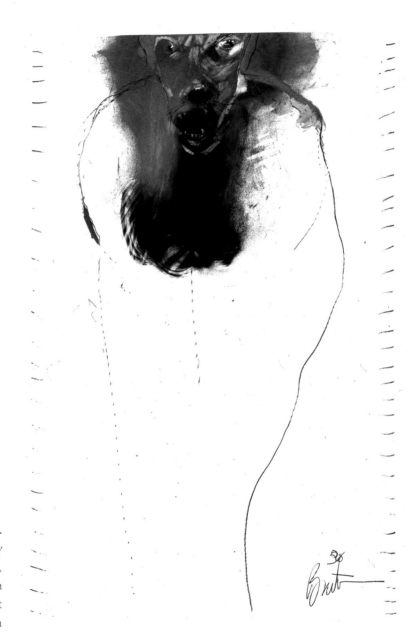

6.4.
"Angry Coyote" by
Rick Bartow (Yurok), 1998,
pastel on paper. Photograph
courtesy of Froelick Adelhart
Gallery, Portland, Oregon

valued for his ability to extend and perfect tradition, not shatter it. (Krantz 1989:23)

In the text of the interview, however, Haozous spoke about the loss of tradition, and about his ironic reconstruction of "Indianness."

I use international concepts that the Europeans attributed to Native Americans when they first met them, such as the Great Environmentalist, the Honest People, the Free People, that certainly are not true today, but did give a foundation, however questionable, on which to base my art. (Haozous in Krantz 1989:24)

Variants of the Indian-as-naturalist stereotype include the Indian-as-spiritual-being and Indian-as-shaman. One author described the graphite and pastel drawings of Yurok artist Rick Bartow (see fig. 6.4) as expressions of a "shamanistic state of consciousness." The writer cited Bartow's manner of overlaying human and animal figures, then smudging the lines between the images, as evidence of the artist's connection to ancient shamanic practices. Bartow persistently disavows the "shaman" label, yet the writer persisted:

While Bartow says he has not actively practiced any specific shamanic or Native American medicine tradition, his art seems to reflect fundamental shamanic and Native beliefs in the transformational, healing powers of animals. (T. White 1988:16)

Where the alternative is an erasure of difference, some artists opt to accept these stereotypes, if only as markers of ethnic pride. When Krantz asked Haozous if his "concepts" are clichés, Haozous defended himself: "They're not clichés, they did exist and they exist today. There's a big difference between a non-Indian and an Indian today" (Haozous in Krantz 1989:25). Flathead painter Jaune Quick-to-See Smith revived the stereotype in her assessment of Bartow's work: "Unlike Europeans, Indian people view themselves as part of nature. They paint the landscape in a tender way, because they feel a part of it. Indians think animals have souls" (Smith in Wasserman 1986:n.p.).

What allows these stereotypes to function as mediators of difference is the common conceit that Native American artists exist in two separate "worlds"—their "native world" and the "modern world." Artists who work in contemporary media, in particular, are "walking in the hazy borderland between worlds" (Allison 1991), translating an "indelible heritage" into a "modern world" (Bensley 1993). As Krantz wrote, "Bob Haozous is a Native American sculptor whose life and work straddles the often diverging worlds of mainstream America

6.5. "Many Moons" (detail) by Doug Coffin (Potawatomi/Creek), 1993, installation. Photograph by Yvonne Bond, Wheelwright Museum of the American Indian, Santa Fe

and his Indian heritage" (1989:23). In the Indian world, there is "no word for art." In the "modern" world, art is produced for art's sake, and cultural baggage is left at home. These ideas, rooted in the ideology of the dominant society, have been appropriated by tribal artists for their own purposes. Together they constitute what Apache anthropologist Nancy Mithlo calls the "Top Indian Art Clichés." In a paper titled, "Is There Really No Word For Art in Our Language?" (1995), Mithlo described how her Native students use these clichés to "escape much tougher questions" (1995:2). This is a dangerous practice because it implies that the "continuation of native identity is not dynamic or changing to present circumstances" (1995:3).

Many critics have a particularly difficult time with political art, in part because it defies all of the above strategies by directly addressing the ways in which Native Americans and their art have been, and continue to be, received by the dominant society. Political art aims to provoke reaction—or at least cause discomfort—by implicating the viewer. In accordance with the mores of late-twentieth-century political correctness, critics tend to avoid the point of direct confrontation by describing events that are general or historic rather than specific or personal. In a review of "Legacies: Contemporary Art by Native American Women," a group show at the College of New Rochelle in New York, a local newspaper columnist wrote, "[t]he overwhelming impression of this exhibit is of peoples who are, understandably, still angry over the American government's attempts to rob them of their identities" (Gouveia 1995:5C). This was the writer's solitary nod to the prevailing attitude of an exhibit in which Cherokee artist Joanna O. Bigfeather stretched small white christening dresses on birch bark frames, representing "Indian children being ripped open and splayed in order to skin them of their cultural roots and to force the dominant society's idea of education and civilization upon them" (Osburn Bigfeather 1995:5).

Some critics cannot entirely conceal their discomfort. William Zimmer's review of "Legacies," which appeared in the *New York Times*, provoked a negative reaction from several of the participating artists because of its patronizing tone: "American Indians are fortunate in that they have a tradition that is of vital importance to them—and at least romantically appealing to the rest of us" (Zimmer 1995:20).[12] Shan Goshorn's photographs of Indian images in American advertisements were intended to demonstrate how this romantic appeal can turn into racial typecasting. Zimmer's reaction to Goshorn's work was flippant and insensitive: "Certainly Crazy Horse Malt Liquor is offensive, but who can really begrudge the Cleveland Indians their grinning imp?" (ibid.).

Here Zimmer's complaint is not about the

quality of the artwork, nor the efficacy of Goshorn's photographs in conveying her political message, but about the nature of the protest itself. In the context of a national debate over the use of racist images to promote professional sports teams, the critic's remarks were inappropriate. In an exhibition review, they are doubly so. Zimmer's review also reveals a remarkable level of ignorance about the circumstances of production and the criteria for evaluation of political art.

When it comes to Native American art, most critics hedge around their charge to evaluate. They hide behind the clichés of alterity, knowing that for the majority of their audience, these clichés will resonate with the truth of an imagined Indian. W. Jackson Rushing is one of a small number of writers who has ventured to evaluate. In some circles this makes him brave, in others, foolhardy, but to my mind his is the first sensible writing, in many cases, on contemporary Native American artists and artwork. This is not just because he knows how to critique the work he reviews, but because he is critical. Rushing is knowledgeable about tribal histories and cultural references, but he holds contemporary tribal art to the standards of the art world in which it strives to move. In other words, he is not afraid to cast a negative judgment, occasionally, when he feels a work is weak or incomplete.

In reviewing "Many Moons," an exhibit of Doug Coffin's new work installed in 1993 at the Wheelwright Museum in Santa Fe (see fig. 6.5), Rushing described the large totemic sculptures in terms of their overall appearance and emotional impact, explaining specific tribal references the average viewer might have missed. He then proceeded to evaluate the installation, both as a whole and as a collection of individual works, in terms of aesthetic quality to the trained Western eye (which, after all, is the eye of most potential consumers):

> I found *Moon Serpent* to be an ungainly object, an ineffective use of the space, and not very well crafted. . . . [T]he seams of the serpent's spine, where glass and metal came together, are rough and unfinished, and the overall image is almost a caricature. (1994b:30)

According to Rushing, the "ersatz" quality of this and several other poles suggested that the work "is not yet fully resolved." Nevertheless, as "an ensemble of objects [the poles] do establish a compelling presence in the gallery, one that depends on the interplay of reflected and refracted light and the poetry of symbols and symbolic materials" (1994b:31).

Rushing, who describes himself as a "white guy from Texas," has little tolerance for the clichés of alterity. Artists don't live in two worlds, they face challenges and histories that vary by tribe, gender, generation, and individual circumstance. The challenge in writing about Native American art is to recognize areas of difference, as well as areas of merging social and cultural practices, as they coexist within and influence the nature of our shared modernity. The goal, as I see it, is the normalization of the relationship between Native and non-Native American arts, a move made all the more urgent by multiculturalism's entrenchment of Native American minority status. As Kay WalkingStick wrote, without critical discussion multiculturalism becomes "just another way to segregate artists" (1992:15).

As long as Western eyes are guiding the decisions of institutional and individual collectors, Native American artists deserve fair and sophisticated treatment by Western aesthetic standards. Anything less recalls the patronizing contests of past Southwestern Indian fairs, where non-Native American judges huddled around baskets and pots pointing out signs of cultural corruption. There is another compelling reason for a fair and sophisticated critique of Native American art: the exposure of racialist attitudes in Western art institutions. Many elite art institutions excuse their exclusion of Native American art on the basis of inferior quality. If artists excluded from important exhibits fare well at the hands of critics who know how to evaluate Native American art, continued exclusion on the basis of quality will be difficult to sustain.

IN OLD ORAIBI on the high mesa in Arizona, the oldest settlement in the Western hemisphere, a Buick pulls up, a tourist and his wife get out and go into a small broken down store and ask about rugs. Old Hopi women with grey braided hair sit around weaving, looking up once then eyes back down. Wikvaya ("one who brings"), a young Hopi, comes into the store and stands in a corner staring at the tourists making them nervous enough to leave. Wikvaya follows them outside and approaches them before they reach the car. He asks them if they want to buy a Kachina doll. They hadn't thought about Kachinas, what they mainly wanted was a rug, but at this point any souvenir of the trip would be good enough. The tourists get in their car expecting to follow Wikvaya in his but instead Wikvaya gets in the front seat right along with them. A real live Indian riding in their car. Wikvaya points out the way and they follow his instructions. Down through the small tar paper shacks and huts along a bumpy dirt road. The man would like to carry on some bit of conversation but can't think of anything to say. The woman is concentrating on keeping her right leg from touching Wikvaya's left leg. Wikvaya could care less about any of it. He just stares out at the village with night black eyes. The road twists and turns until it looks like there's no more houses in sight and the man begins to panic. "What if he's taken us out here to murder us? He probably hates white people. After all you can't blame him. All those years of oppression."

Thus begins Sam Shepard's *Left Handed Kachina*, a short story published in 1973, before Shepard won the Pulitzer Prize for drama. The man and woman in the story buy a kachina from Wikvaya, then return to their home in New York City. One afternoon, the man puts on a record of traditional Hopi songs and sits down to admire his new possession. Suddenly, the kachina tumbles from its shelf. As the man rushes to pick it up, he feels his right hand getting cold, his left hand getting hot. Hallucinating, he sees a green snake sliding toward him, fangs out and head weaving from side to side. The sensation in his hands intensifies, and he starts howling and moving like a dog around the apartment. Finally, rain pours from the ceiling, thunder cracks the plaster and lightning rips through the furniture. As the apartment is transformed into a corn field, the man's wife arrives home, accidentally steps on the kachina, then turns to see her husband, wet and shaking on the floor.

The story is fictional but it illustrates real ideas about Native Americans, cultural difference, and power. In the manner of other postwar experimental artists, Shepard preys on the ironies of popular culture and the American dream, evinced here by the urban couple's search for an authentic souvenir of their trip to the Southwest. Shepard's flat prose reveals the absurdity, and finally the tragedy, of white interest in Indian culture.

All collections of Native American objects assembled by non-Native American collectors "embody something of the interface between the Indian and non-Indian world" (Gordon 1988:18). Constituted of objects excised from their original contexts, the collection represents, and sometimes even replaces, the relationship between Native and non-Native Americans. At the same time, the physical process of collecting generates a special kind of relationship between non-Native American collectors and Native American "collecteds." Literary scholar Leah Dilworth suggests that this relationship is analogous to the relationship between representers and the represented insofar as it is "based on consumption and appropriation rather than on communication between subjects" (Dilworth 1996:8).[1] In this chapter, I investigate the nature of the relationship between non-Native American collectors and Native American "collecteds," and the dynamics of its production and reproduction.

■

We like to think of nature and other societies as being outside of historical time and beyond the boundaries of our own cultural experience. . . . But this exteriority of nature and otherness is mainly fictional as modernity expands and draws every group, class, nation and nature itself into a single framework of relations.

—*Dean MacCannell in* The Tourist
(1989 [1976]:77)

Crossing cultural boundaries is at once exciting and dangerous, satisfying and disturbing. And yet, the cross-cultural process, as art critic Lucy R. Lippard called it, is a "recalcitrant, elusive subject" (1990:3), especially in the context of art worlds, whose hegemonies tend to absorb, rather than reveal, human difference. Many Western collectors experience the collecting of non-Western objects as a crossing of cultural, and perhaps even psychological and spiritual, boundaries. Susan Vogel, a former curator of the Museum for African Art in New York City, recalled a businessman who told her that "African art was the closest he would ever come to God" (1988:5). "African art is said to reach deeper into the intimate emotions," Vogel explained, "and to expose more disturbing psychological truths than any art created before the twentieth century."

For Vogel's collectors, the power of African art resides in its alterity: an essential human difference believed to separate the collectors and the collecteds. This difference is so perfectly contained by the collected objects that actual human contact is deemed unnecessary, and possibly even detrimental, to the collecting experience. According to Vogel, many collectors of African art feel that it is not enlightening to visit the African continent. There the "sweaty reality of use and the sense of things recently removed from their origins" could disrupt a collector's vision of aesthetic jewels plucked from a primitive land (1988:4). One collector admitted that "if Adidas sneakers and Sony Walkmen were absent from the Ivory Coast, I might reconsider my position, but, at present, my romantic vision of pre-colonial Ivory Coast is too fragile to tamper with" (Leyden in Vogel 1988:58).

Native American objects exude a similar kind of power for their collectors. Like Vogel's collectors of African art, most of the collectors of Native American art I interviewed for this project espoused romantic or exotic views of Native American people. But my collectors differed from Vogel's collectors in that they nearly always expressed interest in visiting tribal lands and meeting Native American people.[2] One explanation for this difference might be that Native Americans are more accessible to American collectors. But even if collectors of Native American art are more likely to visit tribal communities, their interactions with Native Americans are so heavily structured by the marketplace and preconceived notions that they rarely yield new information.

American ideas about Indians being more spiritual, romantic, or savage than other peoples generate stereotypical representations of Native Americans in history texts, Hollywood films, and tourist literature. These representations, in turn, reinforce preconceived notions. The cycle is so powerful that it can withstand repeated personal experiences with "real" Indians. As anthropologist Joan D. Laxson discovered in her work on tourism in the Southwest, "[s]tereotypes tend not to be modified by contradictory experiences" (1991:374). To make matters worse, Native American artists may unwittingly support these stereotypes by performing as they are expected (Evans-Pritchard 1989). On both sides, ideas about the Other structure cross-cultural interactions by creating expectations and thus providing models for behavior. The process is dialogic: stereotypes of Anglo consumers and Native American artists inform interactions, while these same interactions, especially brief economic exchanges, serve to reinforce stereotypes.[3]

Problems that arise in the course of cross-cultural communication frequently function to reinforce essential notions of difference. Stories about the difficulty of communicating with Native Americans abound in the reflective writings of non-Native American anthropologists, art historians, dealers, and museum curators. At the core of these stories lies a unique concept of time and order widely known as "Indian time." Although the phrase's exact origin is uncertain, some folklorists believe it may have been coined in the 1960s at the Haskell Indian Junior College in Lawrence, Kansas. A list of slang words current at the school during this time period includes "Indian time," which is explained as a defiant reaction to the confining nature of "white man's time":

The Indian considers that the white man is a slave to time. This view is confirmed for the student when he discovers that classes begin at predetermined hours. However, the Indian does not like to feel bound in this way; that is why he is not embarrassed when he is late for an appointment by white man's standards, for he kept the appointment by Indian time which could be defined as some *unspecified time* following a *specified time*. (Dundes and Porter in Coe 1986:31)

By today's standards of scholarship, this definition, and perhaps even the concept itself, would be considered offensive, a manifestation of the primitivism that has shaped so many representations of tribal peoples. In my experience, the assumptions made about tribal people operating on "Indian time" often border on racism. When communication does not proceed according to Anglo cultural norms, Native Americans are often perceived as irresponsible, lazy, or simply intractable. In a Santa Fe art gallery I overheard a non-Native American manager commiserating with a client about a certain Native American artist's lack of punctuality. What began as a joke quickly expanded into a sweeping generalization: "Well, they're all on Indian time. There's no sense of time for them, actually." On a different occasion, more explicit complaints were made regarding Indian artists' failure to arrive on time for appointments. When they did arrive, they "brought their whole families with them, screaming kids and all, and always needed to use the bathroom as soon as they arrived." (No consideration was given to the fact that artists traveling from remote areas of the Navajo reservation, in particular, drove five or six hours to reach Santa Fe, where they generally had no place to stay and little cash to spend.)

Class is certainly a powerful divider in the Native American art world. But when disparities that arise from differential access to technology and economic opportunities are misinterpreted as inherent cultural differences, the conservative argument for a "culture of poverty" is invoked. This serves two purposes: it eliminates personal responsibility for unequal power relations and the resulting situations of social suffering, and it transforms a moral dilemma into an intellectual game.

The apparent unsuitability of tribal people for city life is reinforced when urbanites visit Indian reservations, with their apparent lack of laws and modern technology. A saleswoman at a different Santa Fe gallery told me that clients ask her as many questions about reservation life as about the pottery for sale. "People come in from the reservations and are just flabbergasted by the conditions," the saleswoman said. "Some lady actually asked me, 'How could something so beautiful come from such a poverty-stricken hovel?'"

With more than half of the gallery's artists hailing from local reservations, this particular saleswoman made an effort to educate customers on tribal histories and cultural differences: "I explain the economics of Native Americans ... [and that] people are different, they come from different worlds, and how you judge something, that may not be their priority."

Contemporary Native American artists cleverly recycle the stereotypical markers of ethnic difference into what has evolved into the pan-tribal phenomenon of "Indian humor." Urban Indians who wear watches and are fully aware of the scheduling constraints of the modern capitalist world will explain their tardiness with the joke, "I'm running on Indian time today." When I arrived late to an interview, I was greeted with a mocking smile and the sarcastic pronouncement, "I didn't know this was on Indian time." Some artists don't find "Indian time" funny, however, especially if it adversely affects their careers. A well-known artist told me the story of his dealings with the Institute of American Indian Arts (IAIA) museum, where he was invited to exhibit his mixed-media sculptures. According to this artist, the museum staff operated on "Indian time" and generally behaved in an unprofessional manner. Their most egregious offense was failing to print and mail announcements on time. As a result, this artist said, he would never again exhibit at this museum, despite the fact that he is an alumnus of the

Institute and an advocate of Native-run galleries and museums.

For non-Native American participants in the Native American art world, the concept of "Indian time" serves as tangible proof of the cultural difference they hope and expect to find in tribal people. Whether or not it is rooted in real cultural difference, "Indian time" has been incorporated into a larger complex of stereotypes, where it functions to obscure the modernity of contemporary tribal peoples. The image of Native Americans as premodern is so popular that consumers are surprised—and sometimes even disappointed—when tribal subjects fail to uphold it. Navajo painter BY described a recent encounter with clients at a gallery opening in Germany:

BY: The last time I had a show [in Germany], it was stuffed with people. Everybody had come to see me, the Navajo artist.

M: What kinds of things did they say?

BY: I have to tell you what I looked like first. [laughter] I went dressed in these real nice clothes, some designer label, something mainstream from Dillard's, and I had hair about this length [to her chin], and it was all dyed blue. So I had this electric blue-colored hair, it was kind of that color, I mean bright blue, I showed up looking like that. And I arrived, and people were like, "Where's the artist? Where's the artist?" When I was introduced, people's jaws just dropped. They said, "This is the Indian?" And they all left soon after that. They were so disappointed I didn't look like their expectations, what they read about and what they see in the books of Native people. . . .[T]hey expected me to show up in this buckskin dress, with my hair flowing. They didn't get that, and they were so disappointed.

American dealers of contemporary art report similar reactions when their clients encounter Native American artists. Chicago gallery owner Jan Cicero started exhibiting the work of contemporary Native American artists in 1990, and since then she has become a major advocate of Native American painting and sculpture. Cicero reported mixed reactions to her first all-Native American exhibit: some viewers were surprised that Native American artists could produce work without reference to stereotypically Indian images; others were disappointed that the stereotypical images were missing. According to Cicero, works by Rick Bartow, Duane Slick, Mario Martinez, Truman Lowe, and Emmi Whitehorse were "very well received by my regular clients, who said, 'This isn't Indian art, this is real art.' Others were disappointed and said, 'This isn't Indian art, there aren't any Indians or feathers'" (Cicero in Teters 1997).

The collector's reluctance to part with exotic stereotypes not only obscures the modernity of contemporary tribal people, but ensures their disappearance as human subjects (Dilworth 1996:8). Relegated to the silence of pre-modernity, living artists are transformed into objects, like mannequins in a museum diorama. In this way, Native American artists are literally collected, their very bodies merging with their artworks to form a product that is biologically and aesthetically "Indian." This collapsing of the tribal and the individual, the biological and the aesthetic, further reduces meaningful personal contact between the collector and the collected because it completes the essentializing of human difference.

▪

Post-structuralists recognize that there is nothing "essential" about cultural difference. And yet, in the course of experience and its remembrance, differences arising from specific cultural and practical constraints are essentialized in a language rife with the descriptors and symbols of alterity. By translating this language, and by analyzing the process of translation and the generation of meaning, we can begin to comprehend the production and reproduction of difference.

In art worlds, translation can refer to the work of the artist, who visualizes the emotional, or the work of the critic, who verbalizes the visual, or the work of curators and collectors, who, by recontextualizing objects, endow them with new and highly personal properties. As Pierre Bourdieu wrote, an art work is a symbolic object that "derives not only its value . . . but also *its significance and truth* from those who receive it just as much as from the man who produces it" (1971:168). In multicultural art worlds, the process of translation assumes additional significance as the space in which cultural difference is negotiated. In the words of Homi K. Bhabha, who wrote an essay for the Whitney Museum's 1993 Biennial Exhibition catalog, difference is negotiated, not fixed, and it is in the process of negotiation that we need to look for meaning: "What is theoretically innovative, and politically crucial, is the need to think beyond narratives of origin . . . and to focus on those moments or processes that are produced in the articulation of 'differences'" (62–3). In other words, cultural meaning is constituted by the act of translation, not prior to it.

Bhabha's attention to translation was appropriate in the context of the 1993 Biennial because this exhibit highlighted the work of minority artists. According to the head curator, selected works exemplified the direction of art in the 1990s because they each presented a specific point of view (e.g., lesbian or African-American) that was grounded in some sort of communal identity. Historically, this kind of art has been

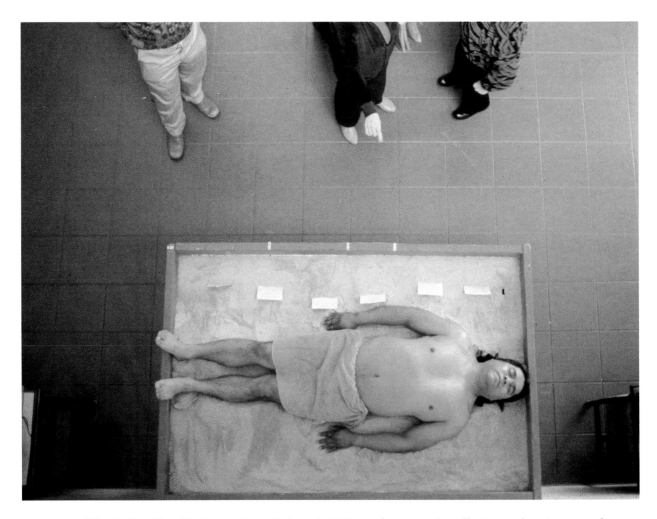

7.1. "The Artifact Piece" by James Luna (Luiseño), 1987, performance/installation at the Museum of Man, San Diego. Photograph courtesy of the artist

relegated to the margins, or to themed exhibits. According to hegemonic reasoning, its intellectual content voided its aesthetic value, and its positionality limited its art-historical significance. This logic excluded, and continues to exclude, many contemporary Native American artists from powerful mainstream arts institutions, like the Whitney. By the Whitney's new (and undeniably politically correct) standard, however, minority artists had their fingers on the pulse of America. As "borderline" artists, they were charged with the important task of translation, of "perform[ing] a poetics of the open border" (Bhabha 1993:64). Bhabha suggested that this performance, this "staging of cultural difference" (1993:69), occurred in the space between representation and community. The simultaneous attendance of different communities introduced the possibility of multiple, and perhaps contradictory, meanings.

Where translation refers to the reinscription of the past, it is an accurate descriptor of much contemporary Native American art. The two Native American artists included in the 1993 Whitney Biennial were James Luna (see fig. 7.1), a Luiseño performance artist, and Jimmie Durham, a Cherokee who works in multiple media. In their work, these men actively reinscribe personal and tribal pasts. Their art "does not merely recall the past as social cause or aesthetic precedent; it renews the past, refiguring it as a contingent 'in-between' space, which inno-

vates and interrupts the performance of the present" (Bhabha 1993:68). The process of artmaking is not an act of nostalgia, but of necessity, insofar as the survival and sovereignty of tribal peoples rely on the rewriting of histories.

Translation can also refer to a synchronic crossing of cultural borders.[4] This kind of translation is not only "provisional," as Walter Benjamin famously stated, but also "imperialistic," as Edmund Carpenter wrote, "at best producing a creative hybrid, but more frequently destructive, turning what is translated into hash or comedy or a mirrored image of the translator" (1972:33). This notion of translation is more appropriately applied to the work of the critic, and by extension, to the work of anthropologists, museum curators, historians, dealers, and collectors, all of whom have acted as interpreters and representers of Native American art.

By focusing on individuals instead of institutions, Bhabha elided the problem of power. But even the process of artistic production, particularly the artist's communication of intent to his or her audiences, is mediated by institutional power. Most Native American artists would agree, I think, that the Biennial's inclusion of Luna and Durham was significant, regardless of the curator's reason for being interested in minority artists. But a recurring complaint of contemporary Native American artists is that their position is established not *by* them, but *for* them, by non-Native American critics and curators. In this case, it was the staff and board of the Whitney. In determining who was speaking from what (marginalized) position, these people were exercising their power as the agents of a powerful institution, one whose previous selection criteria effectively excluded ethnically positioned artists.

Some contemporary Native American artists would prefer that their work remain untranslated. As Charlotte Townsend-Gault wrote in relation to Native Canadian artists, translation may be "withheld" in order to maintain cultural boundaries (1995b:91). This notion of withholding information is not new. Artisans in the Southwest who make cultural souvenirs (e.g., sandpaintings) for tourists typically alter or omit one element of the design in order to protect its power. In the case of contemporary painting and sculpture, protection might take the form of a visual code comprehensible only to those with special knowledge. One example of this practice is Edgar Hachivi Heap of Birds's word drawings, in which precisely crafted texts challenge the viewer's cultural capital.

In their haste to recast contemporary Indian art as expressions of an avant-garde aesthetic, some writers have misinterpreted strategies for boundary-maintenance as markers of postmodernism. There is an unspoken assumption among the rhetorically chic, it seems, that contemporary Native American painting and sculpture is postmodern by dint of its inclination to pastiche, its

positionality, and its political reappropriation of history. Gerhard Hoffman (1987) deemed contemporary Native American art accidentally postmodern, an essentially "primal" art seized by the movement toward pluralism in the arts. Allan J. Ryan saw evidence of postmodernity in Canadian artists' use of the "trickster shift," a process in which the traditional Trickster character is employed in ironic ways to shift the viewer's perspective (1995:11). Joseph Traugott (1992) interpreted the combination of "high and low [art] elements" in the work of Bob Haozous and Felice Lucero-Giaccardo as postmodern because "[t]hese contradictions reflect the discontinuity of living within two cultural systems based upon antithetical social and aesthetic philosophies" (1992:42).

While these readings offer insight into aesthetic strategies, they gloss the fact that circumstances of production and consumption are still firmly tied to the unequal power relations of modernity. As in so many early-twentieth-century accounts of tribal life, the problems of power are concealed by the occlusion of history. When Yuxweluptun draws pure tribal figures in a polluted post-industrial landscape, he is not—according to the critics—commenting on colonialism, but linking "pre-modern tribal life" to contemporary experience (Linsley 1995:23). Decades of consciousness-raising are erased when Yuxweluptun's *Haida Hotdog* (1984) is interpreted as ethnic Pop Art. Like other translations, postmodernism is part of the language of dominance. To be sure, it is more current than the language of cultural primitivism, and more sophisticated than the language of popular culture. But because it privileges the abstract over the real relationships between people from different classes and cultures, it fails to engage the problems of a discourse shaped by primitivist imagination and imperialist politics. In the words of feminist scholar Caren Kaplan, art-writing becomes a form of "theoretical tourism . . . where the margin becomes a linguistic or critical vacation, a new poetics of the exotic" (in Lippard 1990:9).

■

You think of us now
when you kneel
on the earth,
turn holy
in a temporary tourism
of our souls.

—excerpt from "For the White Poets
Who Would Be Indian," by Wendy Rose
(in Vizenor 1995b:273)

Collectors do not like to think of themselves as tourists, the implication being that touristic interest in Native American art and culture is less serious, less informed, and almost certainly lower budget. Still, tourism provides the physi-

cal context for many of the interactions between non-Native American collectors and Native American collecteds. Tourism also provides an insightful theoretical model for understanding the translations and exchanges that occur throughout the collecting process. In sociologist Dean MacCannell's definition of tourism, "reality and authenticity are thought to be elsewhere: in other historical periods and other cultures, in purer, simpler life-styles" (1989 [1976]:3). This "elsewhere" is experienced through sightseeing, a "ritual performed to the differentiations of society" that functions to "overcome the discontinuity of modernity" by "incorporating its fragments into unified experience" (1989 [1976]:13).

Collectors, including tourist-consumers, literally incorporate the "fragments" of other cultures into their experience of modernity when they acquire Native-made objects. At home the souvenir, that logical consummation of the sightseeing experience, signifies a successful encounter with the Other. Exotic souvenirs, like Sam Shepard's Hopi kachina, serve as both specimens and trophies (Stewart 1993:147). As discussed in chapter 3, the journey to the source is a vital part of the collecting process. Like anthropologists who gain admittance to sacred ceremonies, collectors who travel to reservations are rewarded with experiences (and objects) that seem to be more authentic, and thus more powerful, than those available to the general public. But even reservation experiences can be constructed, or "staged," in MacCannell's words. In fact, some tourist experiences are strategically constructed to conceal private or sacred information while satisfying the tourist's desire for authenticity.[5]

Research on tourism in American Indian communities generally explores the social and economic effects of visitors on the host community. Among the positive effects of tourism are economic growth and increased self-esteem (Browne and Nolan 1980, Sweet 1991); among the negative effects are the loss of privacy and the reinforcement of negative stereotypes (Lujan 1993, Laxson 1991, Evans-Pritchard 1989). Carol Chiago Lujan's study of her hometown[6] of Taos Pueblo, New Mexico, reveals a more dynamic situation in which the host community exerts power in deciding which aspects of cultural life to reveal or conceal. Lujan's report assumes a tone at once more personal and more political than reports by other, non-Native American scholars. She starts by emphasizing her tribe's long history of resistance to "unsolicited cultural change" (1993:104), then likens contemporary tourism in Taos Pueblo to the sixteenth-century Spanish invasion. This powerful comparison is elaborated in a statement made by one of her informants:

> When every effort was made to wipe out our culture and religion, we made adjustments to insure that there was an outward showing of compliance. We managed to keep our religion and culture going (underground, as it were) so we were able to survive the Spaniards. So too are we able to survive the tourists and culture they represent. (unidentified Taos Pueblo member in Lujan 1993:101)

Here tourists are likened to the conquistadores, enemy agents to be held off at all costs. But unlike the conquistadores, tourists support the economy of the pueblo to such an extent that most residents accept tourism as necessary to their survival. This paradox is present in many tribal communities, but it is especially evident at Taos Pueblo, where tourism generates a majority of the Pueblo's annual income[7] and tourists have long been allowed to mingle with residents.[8]

Contemporary Native American historians (e.g., Lomawaima 1994) have described how tribal people survived invasion and the subsequent assault of assimilation policies by "going underground," as the above-mentioned informant phrased it. Religious or spiritual activities, in particular, had to be concealed from public view where they were banned by the state. One strategy of resistance was to schedule these activities around the permitted Christian or American secular holidays, such as the Fourth of July, so they would be less noticeable to government agents. As Lujan explained, "Pueblo Indians learned to comply outwardly with forced Christianity while discreetly continuing to practice their religion and lifestyle" (1993:104).

Faced with the modern challenge of tourist invasion, Pueblo people continue the practice of concealment as a strategy to maintain personal privacy and protect tribal traditions, especially religious traditions. In Taos, the most obvious application of this strategy is the annual closing of the Pueblo to all tourists during the month of February, initiated by the Pueblo governor in 1989 (Lujan 1993:113).[9] In addition, sections of the Pueblo are closed to tourists throughout the year. These measures are deemed necessary for the maintenance of cultural integrity, despite the loss of tourism revenues.

Tribal artists whose products and bodies are the objects of non-Native American desire may employ similar strategies of concealment in the processes of production or public presentation. For example, Zuni carvings made for external markets often look identical to fetishes made for internal use, but they differ in one crucial aspect: they have not been blessed by a Zuni priest. This does not stop consumers from endowing the small carvings with special powers, however (Snyder 1993:A1). Likewise, artists who sell their wares under the portal at Santa Fe's Palace of the Governors will change out of

jeans and flannel shirts into more "traditional" (stereotypical) clothing and jewelry before their customers arrive. This not only increases sales but it allows the artists to conceal their personal style and thus protect their privacy.

At the ethnic spectacles that pass for art markets, artists understand and often take advantage of the fact that sales are dependent on the image of "Indianness" they project. In private, however, artists scorn tourists and collectors alike for their ignorant expectations. Tribal anthropologist FH is a longtime judge and volunteer at Santa Fe's annual Indian Market. He counts among his close friends many Indian artists and non-Indian collectors, and over the years has had numerous opportunities to observe their interactions. In his opinion, most of the communication that occurs at Indian Market is very superficial:

FH: I've sat in booths, talking to artists, you know, sitting behind the counter, sitting with them and talking with them, so I know what kind of reaction they [artists] have. [Collectors] will just wander by, and just look and smile, and they may ask the price of something, or try something on.

M: Do they ask if artists live on reservations?

FH: Yes, they ask those usual kinds of questions.

M: How do the artists handle it?

7.2. Untitled painting by Gerald Nailor (Navajo), 1937, gouache on illustration board. Photograph courtesy of the Museum of the Indian Arts and Culture/Laboratory of Anthropology

FH: Most of them are very gracious. I mean, they're not going to be rude, for the most part. You'll run into some who are, they get fed up with it after a while, and I don't blame them, but this is how they're going to get their money.

 M: Do [the artists] make jokes to each other about the customers?

FH: Oh yes, well, they speak in their own languages, of course, many of them, and they'll talk about people that are standing right there, or walking by. [Laughing] They do that all the time.

■

Resistance to the patronizing processes of collecting has shifted in the past few decades from a primarily private behavior to a decidedly public one. Since the late 1960s, scholars and artists have been "calling into question the Western practices of collecting and exhibiting artifacts of non-Western cultures" (Schneider 1996:185). In the context of Native American politics, this resistance is tied to repatriation and the larger movement toward empowerment and sovereignty. Within the Native American art world, the critique of collecting is part of a radical reaction to the colonialist structures of modernity. An ironic yet popular venue for the expression of this critique is the artwork itself.

Considered in relation to the history of Native American resistance, the emergence of po-litical consciousness in the arts occurred relatively late. Art historian J. J. Brody cited Navajo artist Beatien Yazz's *Gallup* (1946) as the earliest example of an "angry, socially conscious picture done by an Indian in modern times" (1971:164). This poster-color painting depicted a realistic border-town scene: tribal people in ceremonial costume parading down Main Street, while Anglos snap photographs and signs in the shop windows warn "No Indian allow" (Brody 1971:164–65).[10] An earlier painting by Navajo artist Gerald Nailor depicts a similarly patronizing scene. Nailor's untitled gouache (see fig. 7.2), which is in the collection of the Museum of Indian Arts and Culture in Santa Fe and dated by the museum to about 1937, shows a traditionally dressed Navajo man holding a rug for a wealthy white couple to inspect. The white man stands aloof, a cigar in his mouth, while the white woman bends to examine the weaving with her magnifying glass. On the other side of the rug the Navajo man's wife waits patiently, head deferentially bowed, children at her feet. While this image is not mentioned by Brody, he would certainly have considered it "socially conscious," if only for its honest depiction of the colonialist nature of collecting.[11]

Contemporary Native American political art continues in the direction of these early paintings, but draws on the strength of the civil rights movement and the inclusive pedagogy of the IAIA's early years. At the Institute, "[m]any young artists . . . saw themselves as warriors of their generation, charged with defending the traditions and beliefs of their people" (R. Hill 1992:72). In the spirit of Red Power and the civil rights movement, IAIA's artist-warriors used their art to express profound anger and disappointment about the persistent discrimination against Native Americans. The newly politicized content of Native American art called for a new visual vocabulary, and many artists working in Western media took advantage of post-Abstract Expressionist techniques—such as collage, repetition, and the employment of text—to expedite the communication of their messages.

Participants in this movement spoke of changes in the content and style of Native American art as a natural development, in tune with other aesthetic and political movements across the country. What many observers saw, however, was a radical uprising that swept through the nation's Indian art community practically overnight:

> The docility that had characterized the first fifty years of Indian painting, the sheer neutrality of content that had made it decorative and descriptive, disappeared in a burst of angry, polemical pictures that use an arsenal of pictorial conventions rarely before explored by Indian artists. (Brody 1971:201–3)

Today, many Native American artists working in the United States and Canada incorporate social or political commentary into their art. Like the state's strategies for annihilation and assimilation, strategies employed by political artists vary from the subtle to the aggressive. Mohawk sculptor Richard Glazer Danay employs humorous satire in his playfully painted *objets trouvés*. Words are the medium of choice for Cheyenne/Arapaho conceptual painter Edgar Hachivi Heap of Birds. Cherokee ceramicist Joanna O. Bigfeather gets right to the point when she lynches the artifacts of colonial history in her violent installation of small white christening dresses. The topics addressed by political artists include colonialism, racism, and environmental destruction. Some of the most powerful images are more personal, however, portraying the bittersweet ironies of communication between people from different cultures and classes, including the interactions that characterize the collecting of Native American art.

Despite their need for patronage, contemporary Native American artists are among the most severe critics of collecting. The most offensive kind of collecting is the removal of historic objects from reservations. Beyond the violent implications of battlefield provenance, there is a pervasive sense of disjuncture, or displacement, a sense that Native American objects are out of place and unable to serve their original functions in the homes of collectors.

Central to this position is the distinction between internal and external markets. Objects created for internal use belong on the reservation, on the homeland, at the center of culture and tradition, while objects created for external markets are forever lost to the living culture. As Cree artist Gerald McMaster explained,

> When you create for the market, the work dies as soon as you finish it because you are severed from it. It takes on a different life if it hangs on somebody's wall or sits in a museum. It's severed. But for a Native community, no. It continues having a relationship with [the artist]. (McMaster in Abbott 1994:5)

Chippewa artist and political activist David Bradley described the metamorphosis of historic objects moving through the market in terms of loss. In their tribal contexts, items such as masks and war bonnets are culturally significant. Once removed, they lose "their real value and their reason for existence. They are flat; they have become the possessions of collectors" (Bradley in Sasser 1983:91). Bradley visualized this concern in his paintings: *The Santa Fe Collector* (1981) is a Whistleresque portrait of an elderly female collector who sits in a chair surrounded by Indian artifacts. Tribal people peer in her window, but the woman remains oblivious to their gazes. Likewise, Bigfeather comments on collectors in her "Collectors Series," in which historic art forms such as ledger books and parfleche bags are recreated in clay, "ossified in the firing process to simulate the spiritually-gutted possessions of non-Indian collectors" (Dubin 1998).

Works by artists like Bradley and Bigfeather challenge non-Native American consumers to examine their actions and intentions. Artists whose work critiques collecting could be seen as "counting coup" on collectors, saying to them: "You may have the financial means to acquire our objects, but you will never have the cultural or spiritual knowledge to use them. In your possession, our objects are mute, transformed from living legacy to the symbols of colonial power relations. *And even though my work embodies this critique, you are still willing to buy it at an exorbitant price!*"

■

The language of cultural difference is convoluted, and, in places, contradictory. Native American political artists attempt to disrupt this language, but the efficacy of their interventions is uncertain. Aesthetic purists tend to cast doubt on the problem-solving potential of political art. As the late critic Clement Greenberg stated, "the artist is charged with making good art. That's it. If it's socially aware, all right, but art solves nothing" (Greenberg in Ostrow 1994:31). Cherokee artist Jimmie Durham might disagree with this statement, but he also complains that Native American political art is not taken seriously:"Native American artists, as artists and as persons responsible to our peoples, have traditionally attempted intervention, but even our attempts are seen as quite minor entertainment" (1992:425). Of course, art can be political in different ways, and artworks that are not political in content can be political in effect. For example, Flathead painter Jaune Quick-to-See Smith has donated prints to benefit the environmental organization Greenpeace, and Nuu-Chah-Nulth carver Joe David has created figural totems, serigraphs, and logos to raise money for the fight against clear-cut logging on his native Meares Island (Mills 1989).

The most significant obstacle to the success of political art is its misinterpretation. Art that deploys stereotypical icons—such as tipis, horses, headdresses, or feathers—in ironic or sarcastic ways is especially vulnerable to misinterpretation. Consumers who associate these images with the imagined Indian of white desire without questioning the political repercussions of representation may fail to understand the work's message. In this situation, images that are intended to critique white desire are transformed into the objects of that desire. Some artists actually take advantage of this confusion by phrasing their discontent in a language that is at once familiar and visually ap-

pealing. One collector told me about his visit to the rural New Mexico studio of a well-known Native American painter whose work addresses the tragedies of environmental destruction and colonial history. After viewing some paintings in progress, this collector asked the artist if the political content of his work ever prevented a sale. The artist replied no, that "people will buy any painting with a horse or a headdress in it, no matter what it means."

Artists who don't employ familiar imagery may encounter rejection in the marketplace, on the grounds of aesthetic viability. A salesman at a Santa Fe gallery recalled one client who asked for a "major" work by Diego Romero, a Cochiti ceramicist whose traditionally formed pots are painted with political scenes. When this salesman sent his client a photograph of a pot "that had to do with Indian gaming and alcoholism, [the client] sent it back because he didn't want to look at a picture of an Indian who was unhappy or [one that] portrayed [Indians] in a negative light. He didn't want that in his home." Not surprisingly, artists whose primary intent is to communicate a political message find this kind of rejection particularly discouraging.

In the course of my research, I did meet a few collectors who expressed genuine interest in the political statements made by particular artists, and who supported these artists by purchasing their work. For these collectors, collecting was not about charity, investment, the display of decorating prowess, or "radical chic" (T. Wolfe 1970); it was about pride, empathy, and respectful support. Still, even empathetic collectors interpreted works according to their own personal histories and sensibilities. JW, a Manhattan high-school teacher, purchased "Broken Fences, Shattered Dreams," a mixed-media wall sculpture by Peter Horne-Serebello, because its message moved her: "It's both an expression of the will to break out, as well as the reflection of the reality of being kept in," she explained. JW and her husband, a businessman, are members of the American Indian Community House Gallery/Museum in New York City and have purchased numerous pieces there. As JW's husband explained, their interest in political art is long-standing and personal:

> I have always liked political art, my whole life. In the sense that, I've always been interested in the expression, in different formats, of cutting-edge political friction. African-American art does that, but also, Native American art does that.
>
> Political art touches both of us. [My wife] comes from South Africa, and in South Africa, you have to respect the underdog. She grew up there well before the change in politics. So you sort of feel, as a humanist, for the underdog. And you have a sense of what fascism is. So [my wife] has

that kind of sense of politics. I have a sense of politics a little bit different, which is a much more analytic one, having grown up in the land of anti-communism. If you can relate to art at all, political art becomes very, very personal, because it deals with feelings we both felt.

Of the political art in her collection, JW's current favorite is "Anthropological Mistake," a plaque from Joanna O. Bigfeather's "Smithsonian Series" (see fig. 7.3). After seeing this work in a group show, JW felt so drawn to it that she made the decision to buy it without asking her husband's opinion, as she usually does. Later, in describing her reaction to the work, she related it to her own life experience:

> I thought it was very powerful, just looking at it very simply, the whole position of it. It has the African side to it, in that it reminds me of the very spiritual, powerful African power figures, because they use the nails to cure whoever their clients are, they put in a nail for their client, into the animal power figure, and pour things over it, so even the shiny part of Joanna's piece is like the libations poured. And it looks like an arrowhead, too, which brings us to the Native American. It's like a mummy, which I think it is supposed to look like.
> Because really what it's representing is

7.3. "Anthropological Mistake" (detail) by Joanna O. Bigfeather (Cherokee), 1995, mixed media (raku, aluminum, nails). Photograph by Margaret Dubin

all those thousands of Native American skeletons in the Smithsonian's closets. So not only the real skeletons, but the closet skeletons. Plus, just as a contemporary piece, I think a lot of life, you need to remember the harshness of it, even if it's not your personal life. But the realities of life, to try and make an impact, and do something. So that's why I like waking up to a piece like that. To just remind me that life isn't just to see how comfortable I can be.

Clearly, collected objects play an important role in the production of cross-cultural relationships. Even the most politically or culturally informed of these relationships reproduces stereotypes, however, because, in the end, collected objects reinforce the collector's sense of self. As collectors differ from one another in their opinions, desires, and intentions, so do their interpretations and manipulations of objects. Artists who attempt to intervene in this process encounter obstacles erected by the marketplace, museums, sanctioned scribes, and other artists.

In the process of negotiating positions for themselves in the art world, contemporary artists are forced to engage in contradictory discourses. In the realm of historic objects, the Western art-world's emphasis on rarity and value is opposed to the tribal emphasis on the authority of ownership and representation. In the realm of contemporary art, the conflicting demands of tribal convention and freedom of expression remain unresolved by the movement toward multiculturalism. As long as the objects created by Native American artists continue to serve both as the symbols of race and the tools with which racial discrimination is attacked, these contradictory discourses will persist.

E p i l o g u e

Imagine yourself suddenly set down surrounded by all your gear, alone on a tropical beach close to a native village, while the launch or dinghy which has brought you sails away out of sight.
—*Bronislaw Malinowski,* Argonauts of the Western Pacific *(1953 [1922]:4)*

To the harried corporate executive, this might sound like a dream vacation. But for the early-twentieth-century anthropologist, this leave-taking marked the start of a long, difficult period of isolation otherwise known as fieldwork. For much of this century, disciplinary tradition has required the anthropologist to journey to a distant and isolated land (in this regard, islands are ideal) inhabited by pre-industrial peoples, creating a situation of heightened human difference that is represented and reconciled in the final field report.

Despite my nostalgic predilection for the traditions of my discipline, the subject of this dissertation required a different approach. The fieldwork I undertook tested not my endurance of physical hardship, but my urban savvy: the ease with which I could maneuver through a vast morass of identity politics while living out of a suitcase. There were no fourteen-hour airplane flights to endure, no trekking through rainforests, no bouts with water-borne diseases—just the unfamiliar geographies of unfamiliar cities and one sweltering summer without an air conditioner on the Upper West Side of New York City.

Although Bronislaw Malinowski is remembered as a functionalist who recognized the complexity of "primitive" life, his vision of the field corresponded to the prevailing human hierarchies of his time: social evolutionism and colonialism. As interpreted by social evolutionists, Charles Darwin's theory of descent with modification cast order upon a planet already segmented into the "savage" and the "civilized." While the "savages" may not have been biologically inferior to the "civilized," they were chronologically anterior in their intellectual and technological development. By this logic, the study of "savages" could provide clues to the origin and development of "civilized" societies. Meanwhile, the geopolitical migrations of colonialism set the stage for relatively safe ethnographic fieldwork in a wide variety of isolated and exotic locations.

Successive reformulations of culture theory and the collapse of colonialism have required "the field" to be radically re-visioned. For some, the anthropological field can no longer exist, because its founding was predicated on colonial power relations. For others, the field is in a state of flux, while the discipline as a whole experiences a "crisis of representation" (Marcus and Fischer 1986:8). As a graduate student about to embark on her first long-term fieldwork, I was less concerned about the fate of the discipline than I was about constructing a fieldsite that could meet the practical requirements of my project. In this brief epilogue I reflect on the aspects of contemporary ethnographic research I found most challenging: the fragmented nature of the field and the difficulty of moving through a landscape held hostage by the politics of identity.

■

Proper conditions for ethnographic work. These, as said, consist mainly in cutting oneself off from the company of other white men, and remaining in as close contact with the natives as possible, which really can only be achieved by camping right in their villages.
—*Bronislaw Malinowski,* Argonauts of the Western Pacific *(1953 [1922]:6)*

The traditional anthropological field was inhabited by people who lived and worked in a "natural" environment. Like animals, anthropological subjects were most appropriately studied in nature, in their native communities. This nature stood in opposition to the industrial spaces of civilized society, whence the anthropologist came. Today we recognize that the traditional fieldsite was not natural at all, but constructed as a "setting for the discovery of difference" (Gupta and Ferguson 1997a:5). The construction of fieldsites allowed bounded geographical areas to be correlated with specific cultural, physical, and linguistic traits. Employment of the "peoples and cultures" paradigm (Gupta and Ferguson 1997b:25) simplified fieldwork by circumscribing the natural fieldsite with clear physical boundaries that dictated research scope and methodology.

Research for this book required a different kind of field, one in which I could study "up" (Nader 1972) as well as "down," "in," and "out."

Because I needed to interview and observe individuals operating in different sectors of the Native American art world, I could not rely on one physical location to provide all my data. Without the luxury of a clear physical boundary to dictate the scope and methodology of my research, I had to develop a model capable of organizing data gathered from a variety of sources in a variety of locations. Through trial and error I found that the most useful model was a kind of pastiche founded in theory (derived from Howard Becker and Pierre Bourdieu), personal experience (from years of attendance at Native American art-world events), and faith (that my training as an anthropologist and my prior experience as a journalist would carry me through the difficult times). My model didn't win the seal of approval from the National Science Foundation, but it did guide my movement from site to site and suggest directions for further inquiries. It also allowed me to incorporate textual data into my fieldnotes without losing site of the knowledge gained through experience.

In its scope and methodology, this book is probably more representative than not of the "new ethnography," which attempts to address the concerns of modern, fragmented, or culturally heterogeneous communities while paying attention to the discursive aspects of cultural representation (Clifford and Marcus 1986). Those who track the trends of the discipline suggest that new ethnography needs a new theory of culture. I disagree. Even if our scope and methodology have changed, the ideological foundation of the inquiry has not: we still seek continuity, and we arrange our fragments to provide it. This is why one fieldsite is no longer enough, because the communities we seek to represent as functioning wholes are dispersed through time and space.

■

. . . as they knew that I would thrust my nose into everything, even where a well-mannered native would not dream of intruding, they finished by regarding me as part and parcel of their life, a necessary evil or nuisance, mitigated by donations of tobacco.
—*Bronislaw Malinowski,* Argonauts of the Western Pacific *(1953 [1922]:8)*

Each fieldsite presents its own unique set of challenges and rewards. One of the most consistent challenges I encountered took the form of flak about my being an anthropologist. This was something I expected: since the renaissance of Indian nationalism in the 1960s, anthropologists have been the subjects of intense criticism from Native American scholars. Early-twentieth-century anthropologists, in particular, are seen as intellectual colonizers whose representations replaced the reality of Indian lives destroyed by conquest. This critique was catalyzed by the

1969 publication of Vine Deloria's *Custer Died For Your Sins*, in which the author connected anthropology to state control over Indian lives: "Behind each . . . policy and program with which Indians are plagued, if traced completely back to its origin, stands the anthropologist" (1988 [1969]:81).

Among contemporary tribal groups, the repatriation of knowledge and representational authority has contributed to empowerment and to the larger movement toward sovereignty. Meanwhile, anthropologists have found themselves being turned away from communities where they or their predecessors had previously been welcome. Anthropologist Peter Nabokov recalled a hostile encounter that occurred in the early 1980s while he was conducting fieldwork on the Crow Reservation in Montana. After going to great lengths to get permission to attend a Tobacco Society dance, Nabokov was surprised to find himself escorted to the door

of the basketball court where the ritual ground had been established. . . . [The event's Pipelighter] introduced himself, and said he didn't want me around. He knew who I was, he said, the guy who wrote *Two Leggings*, and added that they [the Crow tribe] had gotten no royalties from that. Then he stepped back and extended his arm. I almost flinched until I realized he was indicating some far distance. "All this,"

he said, sweeping the entire Crow reservation into the arc of his arm, "all this is copyrighted." (Nabokov 1988:353)

As a former resident of Indian country, I understood the widespread hostility toward anthropologists and constantly worked to reconcile my intentions with the needs and expectations of Native American friends and informants. What I found, however, and could not have predicted, was that most of the flak I encountered came from non-Native Americans who had assumed the role of gatekeepers to the Native American art world. The Anglo owner of an upscale East Coast art gallery cross-examined me for nearly twenty minutes before consenting to discuss her representation of Jaune Quick-to-See Smith, an internationally known Flathead painter. As a gesture of professionalism and honesty in representation, I always offered potential informants a business card that stated my affiliation with University of California, Berkeley's Department of Anthropology (see fig. E.1).

In the privacy of her office, the gallery owner glanced at my card and practically shrieked when she saw the word "anthropology." After determining that I was a cultural anthropologist, not an archaeologist or physical anthropologist, she telephoned Quick-to-See Smith in New Mexico to discuss my request for information. I waited patiently in a chair while the phone conversation moved from casual greetings, to inquiries about family members and recent sales, to the situation at hand. The side of the conversation I heard went like this:

"She's in the anthropology department at Berkeley . . . Yes, she knows Indians are alive. What she's doing is more art history and sociology, so that's cool . . . But she's very white-bread."

Turning to me, the gallery owner asked, "What's that? What did you say?"

To Quick-to-See Smith, she said, "Oh, her father's Jewish." All of a sudden she burst out laughing, then addressed me again, without covering the mouthpiece: "She said you're okay. We'll let you in. You're tribal."

My initial feeling of relief was quickly followed by annoyance. Who was this person to decide whether I could study the Native American art world? Who was she, a wealthy white woman who supported herself with profits earned by selling the work of a Native

American artist, to determine my political aptitude? In retrospect, I understood this interaction as a strategy on the part of the gallery owner to display and protect her status as an "insider" in the Native American art world.

Two thousand miles west and a year later, my encounter with a gatekeeper of another sort proved more challenging. I had driven to a small town north of Santa Fe to interview a Native American sculptor. A renovated church served as the artist's studio, and when I arrived he was sitting on the porch, sharing a bottle of wine with an Anglo friend. His friend, it turned out, was a dealer of historic Native American art who was visiting from Oklahoma. Before entering the studio, I introduced myself as a graduate student in the Department of Anthropology at University of California, Berkeley. The sculptor didn't seem to care, commenting that he knew a couple of anthropologists at the museums in

Margaret Dubin
Ph.D. Candidate
Department of Anthropology

University of California
232 Kroeber Hall
Berkeley, CA 94720

TEL: (510) 642-3391
FAX: (510) 643-8557

E.1

Santa Fe, but this information didn't sit well with the man from Oklahoma.

During the interview, the art dealer remained outside, nursing his glass of wine. He entered the studio only once, to get a new bottle of wine and a light for his cigar. When I was ready to leave, the sculptor escorted me out to the porch. His friend put down his glass and rose from the chair, then suddenly became agitated, grabbing me by the arm and gesticulating wildly.

"Before you go, I've got to get a picture with you holding a caliper to [the artist's] head. You did say you were an anthropologist, right?" When I didn't reply, the dealer repeated his request. He didn't have a camera, of course, but he refused to let go of my arm. A few feet away, the sculptor raised a hand to his mouth and smothered a chuckle.

I started to formulate a response that would explain the history of the discipline, the four fields and Boasian cultural relativism and the recent politicization of scholarship, then decided against it.

"Maybe next time," I replied with a smile, and the men burst out laughing.

■

[The] goal is, briefly, to grasp the native's point of view, his relation to life, to realise *his* vision of *his* world.
—*Bronislaw Malinowski,* Argonauts of the Western Pacific *(1953 [1922]:25)*

The "problem" of conducting fieldwork in contemporary Native America is connected to the challenge of organizing multilocal ethnography. Both situations reflect demographic and ideological shifts that have transformed the "ethnographer's magic" (Malinowski 1953 [1922]:6) into trickery crafted by academic paradigms and sponsored by colonial governments. Assailed for abusing authoritative rhetoric, some anthropologists have answered the call for more "experimental" writing (Clifford and Marcus 1986). Texts produced in this mode are politically safer because they privilege the Self as much as the Other. Unfortunately, this positional switch has allowed some ethnographers to disengage from the intellectual debates that make anthropology a significant academic discipline.

The charge for contemporary anthropologists, as I see it, is to produce texts that acknowledge, explicate—and possibly even challenge—power relations, while not losing sight of cultural processes and the everyday lives of human subjects. Art worlds are informal networks that link institutions to individuals in relationships that shift according to prevailing relations of power. The Native American art world, in particular, has proven to be a rich subject for exploring how cultural processes—such as the construction of ethnic identity and the remembrance of colonialist practice—influence the distribution and exercise of power.

Introduction

1. All the sculptures were eventually sold at various Indian art fairs throughout the year, particularly Eight Northern Pueblos in Santa Clara and Indian Market in Santa Fe. While my friend probably realized greater profit in the end, the lack of steady income prevented him from purchasing much-needed supplies and making payments on his truck.

2. Trading posts have played a significant role in reservation economies for more than a century. Over the years they have evolved from community centers, where reservation residents could pick up supplies and occasionally sell or trade artifacts, to tourist destinations for non-Indian travelers.

3. To protect the privacy of my sources, individuals are referred to by initials that do not correspond to their real names, and some identifying characteristics have been changed. Sources who gave permission to reveal their identity are referred to by their full, real names (see especially chapter 6).

4. This phrase, moved into popular usage by Benedict Anderson (1983), has proven extremely useful for anthropologists working in modern urban fieldsites. As Anderson pointed out, "all communities larger than primordial villages of face-to-face contact (and perhaps even these) are imagined," distinguishable only by "the style in which they are imagined" (1983:15). Like nation-states (Anderson's unit of analysis), art worlds are imagined as politically homogeneous communities, "regardless of the actual inequality and exploitation that may prevail" (1983:16).

Chapter 1

1. For a discussion of the parallel phenomenon in Canada, see Francis 1992.

2. In the Native American Studies section of the Department of Ethnic Studies at the University of California, Berkeley, course listings include "Making History, Making 'Indians,'" taught by Patricia Hilden, and "Native American Simulations," taught by Gerald Vizenor. Both courses explore the role of "invented Indians" in "master narratives of United States history." Both also problematize the more conventional historical overviews the department is required to offer, including "Native Americans in North America to 1900," "History of Native Americans in California," and "Plains Indian History."

3. Gill's premise is that the concept of "Mother Earth," commonly believed to be of prehistoric tribal origin, was jointly constructed by the long history of European-American imagining and the more recent rise of American Indian identity politics. As a conceptual construct, "Mother Earth" falls into the standard repertoire of representations of American Indians. Native political activists' references to "Mother Earth," as in Russell Means's frequently quoted phrase, "Mother Earth will retaliate" (in Gill 1987:1), are less meaningful, according to Gill's logic, because they rely on the imagined affinities of the earth to Indians and of the concept to prehistoric tribal speakers.

Means propagated another popular construct in 1976 when he allowed Andy Warhol to create a series of serigraph portraits of him in stereotypical Plains Indian garb. Means was on trial for murder at the time, and he needed the $5,000 sitting fee to pay his legal costs, according to one account (Hill 1997:49).

4. History has proven this altruism misguided on several occasions, especially when objects deposited in Western museums under the pretext of "preservation" have been adulterated, stolen, destroyed in fires, or otherwise lost. In the United States, Iroquois objects collected in 1849–50 by Lewis Henry Morgan were lost in the "disastrous Capitol fire of March 29, 1911" (Lanford 1994:64). In Europe, the Museum für Völkerkunde packed its most valuable objects—including an extensive North American collection—in crates for safekeeping after Hitler came to power. Some of these crates were buried deep in East German potassium mines, but others were seized by the Soviet army. It took forty years for the collection to be reunited and returned to the museum. Many objects were damaged, and some are still missing (Fienup-Riordan 1996:225).

5. As Diane Fane explains in *Objects of Myth and Memory*, replicas are problem-

atic "in terms of their cultural authenticity and historical significance" because
they were "[s]ummoned into existence
by the collecting process itself" (1991:
27). Documented replicas are useful in
reconstructing tribal histories, insofar
as they point to gaps in extant material
culture at the time of collection. But,
as Fane notes, the very existence of tribal
artisans capable of making replicas ne-
gates the premise of scientific collecting:
the conviction that Indians were a
"dying race."

6. In some cases, dealers also provided access
to contemporary artists. Marvin Cohodas
notes that Otis T. Mason relied on northern California dealers for information on
the weavers featured in his monograph on
Native American basketry, which was
published by the Smithsonian Institution
in 1904 (Cohodas 1992:91).

7. This hierarchy of value was (and still is) reinforced at Indian art fairs, such as Santa
Fe's annual Indian Market, where authenticity is rewarded with monetary prizes
(Mullin 1992:407).

8. As it turns out, the arts were merely in hi-
bernation; four decades later, when art historian Ted Coe ventured into the field to
determine if Native Americans were still
making traditional-style art, the answer was
a resounding "yes" (see Coe's *Lost and*

*Found Traditions: Native American Art 1965–
1985* [1986]).

9. Only in recent years has the promotion
from artifact to art made room for a
greater variety of forms and minimized
the issue of commoditization, at least for
high-end contemporary arts. In a critique
of an exhibit of Navajo rugs woven in the
style of Kenneth Noland's abstract expressionist paintings, the reviewer reminded
her audience that the "commoditization
that has occurred in response to the collector's market should in no way trivialize
the creative impulse of native peoples"
(McGreevy 1993:227). Interestingly, abstract designs are still accorded higher
"art" value than representational designs,
which in the medium of Navajo weaving
are termed "pictorial" and resigned to the
category of "folk art."

10. In anticipation of a massive rejection of
Native spiritual life and its physical accouterments, unscrupulous collectors descended upon reservation communities to
purchase traditional objects. After the
government ban of potlatch ceremonies,
for example, one collector "rushed to [the
Native settlement at New Kasaan, on
Prince of Wales Island in Alaska] in the
hope that the Indians would sell their ceremonial regalia" (Wyatt 1984:22). While
his effort was unsuccessful, many other

collectors profited from the state's suppression of Indian cultural practices.

11. In their unpublished manuscript, Hilden, Huhndorf, and Kalafatic discuss how several tribal consultants were censored by the National Museum of the American Indian (NMAI) because they commented on the unethical circumstances in which several of the museum's objects had been acquired (1995:53).

12. Restrictions on the sale of American Indian objects are so pervasive that some dealers view potential purchases in terms of the laws they might violate. As Santa Fe dealer and collector Kim Martindale explained, "There's archaeological material, religious material, and feathers."

13. One philanthropically minded New York City woman even started her own non-profit foundation to purchase objects for repatriation to tribes. The foundation, founded and directed by Elizabeth Sackler, also accepts donations of objects from collectors, who receive tax write-offs in return for their good will.

14. Repatriation may reverse historical displacements, but it does not erase their effects from communal memory. Repatriated objects are reinserted into the fabric of tribal communities in modern, frequently alien, contexts, such as the cinder block and barbed-wire box that houses repatriated war gods in Zuni Pueblo, or the new tribal museums in Alert Bay and Cape Mudge (British Columbia, Canada) that house repatriated potlatch materials.

Chapter 2

1. The art world I describe crosses national boundaries to include many Native Canadian artists, but for the sake of brevity, I address Native Canadian art only in the context of its circulation within the United States. The situation in Canada parallels that in the United States in many ways, although there has been less direct regulation of contemporary art sales in Canada.

2. The term "blood," a euphemism for race, has been incorporated in an ironic sense into modern pan-Indian vocabulary. In urban Indian communities, for example, "pure" Indians will refer to themselves as "bloods." Ethnically mixed people are often called "breeds," a shortened version of the derogatory "half-breed."

3. For a detailed history of the Indian Arts and Crafts Board from 1935–45, see Schrader 1983.

4. Imported "counterfeits" are still a serious problem for Southwestern tribes, according to an August 1997 *New York Times* article: "Brazilians, Nigerians and Pakistanis weave copies of Apache, Navajo and Pima

baskets. Mexicans weave imitation Navajo blankets. Chinese carve animal fetishes," and Thai and Filipino workers make imitation jewelry (Brooke 1997:A6). One American jewelry manufacturer even convinced a town in the southern Philippines to rename itself "Zuni" in order to evade the trade laws.

5. The Indian Arts and Crafts Association continues its vigilantism by encouraging the enforcement of state and federal laws designed to prevent misrepresentation of Indian products in the marketplace. Artists and dealers who apply to join the organization must be approved by the board of directors, the membership committee, and the members at large. Membership can be revoked if the individual or business does not follow the organization's code of ethics, which requires "honest representation" and "proper identification" of Indian products (Indian Arts and Crafts Association 1994:3).

   The Antique Tribal Art Dealers Association (ATADA), established in 1988, monitors the antique market for forged historic and prehistoric objects, sometimes called "artifakes."

6. This change represents current case law, specifically the 1978 U.S. Supreme Court decision in *Santa Clara Pueblo v. Martinez*, which stated that tribal citizenship could only be determined by the appropriate tribal nation (Harjo 1991). In this case, the Pueblo upheld its custom of refusing to recognize as tribal members the children of a woman who married outside her tribe. The new act gives tribes the option of recognizing an individual as a tribal artisan but not a tribal member. As one Native activist pointed out, this option is the most lenient in federal Indian law: "[o]ther laws require stricter documentation to receive, for example, medical treatment or aid to families with dependent children" (Harjo 1991:n.p.).

7. For a detailed argument supporting this practice, see Sheffield 1997.

8. For a provocative discussion of the "death" of primitivism, see Errington 1998.

9. Both Native and non-Native American people contribute to this discourse, sometimes in tandem. An example of a joint contribution is the "We Have No Word For Art" syndrome (see chapter 7).

10. Today, sophisticated scientific techniques are used to identify fakes. As described in the Metropolitan Museum of Art's 1995 exhibit, "Rembrandt/Not Rembrandt," a combination of X Rays, neutron activation autoradiography, infrared imaging, and microscopic methods helped experts to determine which paintings in the

museum's collection were painted by Rembrandt and which were commonly attributed to Rembrandt but actually painted by his contemporaries.

11. This is the name given to itinerant African art dealers who set up shop in Manhattan hotels throughout the year. According to Lemann, almost all African art enters the United States with these men. "Visits from runners are a daily event at even the very best African art galleries in New York, and the runners, after they've worked New York, usually go on the road in mini-vans, selling from hotel rooms in Chicago, Los Angeles, and other cities" (Lemann 1987:24).

12. The label for one "fake," a sculpture of two bearded male figures carved by a recognized modern Baule artist, stated that the object served no known function in Baule society. The known, of course, is that body of ethnographic knowledge produced by anthropologists, whose reports may have been inaccurate or incomplete. Norick acknowledged that the project of separating "fake" from "authentic" is problematic, but, nevertheless, proceeded, citing the increasing demand for "authentic" pieces. Susan Vogel concurred, calling the standards of authenticity a "seemingly arcane value system" that "rejects whole classes of authentic objects" (1988:4).

Anthropologist Christopher Steiner made an important point when he noted that criteria for authenticity in African art "cut living African peoples off from the market" (1995).

The issue was debated in the press in 1995, when Great Britain hosted a festival of contemporary and historic African art. The Royal Academy sponsored an exhibit of African artworks created before 1900. Elsewhere in London, galleries showed modern artworks, including paintings, photography, and mixed-media installations, prompting the *New York Times* to ask, "Can contemporary African art break with [the] past and still remain African?" (Riding 1995).

13. With the surging popularity of indigenous arts across the globe, this is becoming an international problem. In Australia, two white artists who had been masquerading as Australian Aboriginals were exposed in March 1997. In one case, an elderly white painter named Elizabeth Durack had fabricated the indigenous persona of Eddie Burrup to sell a new series of paintings (Farnsworth 1997:B1).

14. One of the most interesting cases of transculturalism is that of Lelooska, a Cherokee who relocated to the Northwest Coast and learned to carve in the regional style. As with the white carvers mentioned

above, Lelooska's workmanship is considered fine (Strickland 1986:291).

15. In an essay on Native American filmmaking, Hopi producer Victor Masayesva suggests a pan-Indian aesthetic that influences the treatment of motion in film (1994:21). He doesn't explain how this aesthetic might have evolved from tribal (or pre-film) aesthetics.

16. Ironically, many contemporary Northwest Coast artists learn aesthetic traditions from the anthropological record.

17. Traditions can also be invented by patrons to legitimate their collecting activity. For example, easel painting was initiated and encouraged by well-meaning white patrons. The medium was subsequently inserted into a narrative of tradition that functioned, in part, to legitimize white control over Indian creativity. Critics and historians of Native American art wrote about the relationship of easel paintings to historic and prehistoric images, such as rock art, hide paintings, and ledger-book drawings. Contemporary Native American artists may also rely on this invented narrative of continuity, but rarely without a simultaneous critique of the colonialist interference of non-Indian patrons.

18. Today, objects manifesting Native American people's "negotiation of Western artistic and economic systems" are not excluded from exhibitions and markets, but they are frequently marginalized. For example, Tony Jojola's blown-glass vessels are relegated by Santa Fe's Indian Market judges to the category of "Miscellaneous," as are Joanna O. Bigfeather's politically informed ceramic sculptures (see figure 7.3).

Chapter 3

1. Wolfe's musings on the culture of art collecting and leftist politics are more literary than scientific, but in them lie the seeds of truth. In a sociological study of art in New York City homes, David Halle generated statistics that link socio-economic identity and political affiliation to the collection of "primitive" art. Among other things, Halle found that "primitive" (African, Native American, and Oceanic) art was much more popular among the upper-middle and middle classes than among the working classes, and that collectors of "primitive" art were more likely to be registered Democrat than Republican (1993b:142–154).

2. Collecting may absolve patrons of guilt, but it doesn't solve the practical problems of tribal individuals. When anthropologist Rebecca Dobkins interviewed patrons of the late Maidu painter Frank Day, one collector said she purchased Day's paintings as an act of charity. This patron collected

exclusively Native American art, and she explained her preference in terms of a personal altruism: "I feel that is one way they [Native Americans] can retain their dignity and still live in a lifestyle that they want to live in. . . . I buy the art because it helps them financially" (Merrill in Dobkins 1995:201–2). As Dobkins pointed out, patronage "never helped Day to live much beyond the poverty level" (1995:202), but it did encourage him to continue painting.

3. Today, this insider noted, the same baskets could bring $200,000 to $300,000 at auction.

4. In 1995, a new magazine covering the work of living artists started publication. The overnight success of *Indian Artist* was an indication of the continuing popularity of Native American art.

5. Thaw may have been attempting to redress this omission when he invited local tribal elders to speak at the ceremonial opening of the American Indian Wing at the New York State Historical Association's Fenimore House Museum, in Cooperstown, New York. The event celebrated the completion of the $10 million, 18,000-square-foot addition built to house Thaw's collection. A symposium on Native American art and workshops in various traditional Native American crafts were held in conjunction with the open-

ing. In a typically racial division of labor, symposium speakers were non-Native art historians (Steven Brown on the Northwest Coast, Janet Berlo on ledger-book drawings, Evan Maurer on Woodlands spoons and bowls), while workshop leaders were Native American artists (Tom Huff on soapstone carving, Karen Crow on beadworking).

6. Most dealers also fit this description, and when I asked them for help in finding a wider variety of informants, the response I typically received was, "Well, most of my clients *are* middle-class white people." I was, however, able to locate one African-American man who collected contemporary Northwest Coast prints and historic Hopi kachinas ("I was priced out of the market for African art," he explained), and several Native American artists who collected historic material.

7. According to the dealers I spoke with, a similar phenomenon occurs in other specialized sectors of the art market.

8. Collectors accused of buying or trading sacred goods frequently appeal to altruism as justification of illegal or unethical activity. For example, Richard Corrow stated that he was only trying to "preserve" the Navajo Yei B'Chai masks for posterity (see chapter 1). One anthropologist I interviewed told me she had purchased prehis-

toric pottery from pot-hunters (and in the process, engaged in an illegal activity) in order to "keep [the pots] off the black market."

9. African art ranks above other "primitive" arts in this hierarchy. One New York City woman told me that she and her husband had switched their collecting activities from African to Native American art because they found the African art scene too pompous and "white-monied."

10. Admirers and beneficiaries of the Thaws credit their rapid accumulation of important material to awesome connoisseurship: "Few collections of American Indian art have been formed by connoisseurs, such as the Thaws. . . . The Thaws' long-time familiarity with the art world enabled them to educate themselves about American Indian art in a remarkably short period of time" (Vincent 1995:64–65).

11. In most cases, polished silver indicates a preference for cosmetic appearance over preservation. As a preservationist explained, "Any time you polish, you remove part of the silver. Collectors and dealers like to polish their silver because they want it to look nice. General museum practice is to leave it alone unless it's actively deteriorating."

12. The goods tourists purchase are grouped in a special sector of the art market known as "tourist art" or "airport art" (Graburn 1976). This sector, long marked by its reputed "kitschy" combination of low quality and cultural inauthenticity, has only recently been recognized as a "real" category of artistic products, worthy of attention from art historians and museum curators.

13. Of the ethnic arts sold in the United States, those most frequently and intimately associated with "power" are African. The power of African objects arises from their imagined origin in cultural communities that were not only premodern, precapitalist, precolonialist, and pre-Christian, but utterly different (see chapter 7).

14. In a typical affirmation of the hierarchy of "level of engagement," an anthropologist who read this chapter demeaned WF's certificate as a "travel agent gimmick for tourists."

Chapter 4

1. James Clifford borrowed a line of poetry from William Carlos Williams to evoke the prevalent perception of modernity as a condition of "rootlessness" and "cultural incest" in which authenticity is endangered (1988:3–4).

2. While a few of the artists' statements were published in books or articles, most were

recorded during interviews I conducted between 1994 and 1997. Artists who wished to be identified are referred to by name. Artists whose names and identifying characteristics have been changed are referred to by initials.

3. In the interviews quoted throughout this chapter, I am the speaker identified as "M."

4. Earlier in the summer, Lomahaftewa and I had discussed the traditional animosity between Navajo and Hopi people. Lomahaftewa has several Navajo friends and feels the rivalry is generally exaggerated by the media. My comment here was partly in jest, referring to the exaggerated rivalry as well as the stereotypical depiction of Navajo people as the shepherds of Indian country.

5. The polarization of rural and urban spaces is a significant factor in the formation of contemporary tribal identity, but because of space limitations I cannot explore this issue here.

6. Unlike African- or Anglo-American self-taught painters, Native American self-taught painters are not automatically relegated to the category of "folk" artists. In fact, the level of formal education achieved does not seem to have much bearing on an artist's status in the Native American art world. James Lavadour, a self-taught painter who has lived his entire life on the Umatilla reservation in northeastern Oregon, exhibits at prestigious museums alongside Kay WalkingStick, a Cherokee painter who received her MFA at Pratt Institute and teaches in the Department of Fine Arts at Cornell University.

7. For information on the events leading to the founding of IAIA, see Garmhausen 1988, Gritton 1991, and Gritton 2000.

8. According to art historian Joy Gritton (1992), some teachers at IAIA have encouraged students to create images palatable to the market, a practice that conflicts with IAIA philosophy. While this may be true for certain teachers at certain times, the instructors I interviewed in 1996 seemed more disturbed by the colonialist aspects of the local art market than lured by its commercial potential.

9. For an excellent discussion of modernism in American art, see Ashton 1982.

10. Most artists with tribal heritage identify themselves as Native American, but some choose not to. GW is, to the best of his knowledge, a full-blooded Navajo. Adopted at birth by an Anglo couple, he grew up in middle-class comfort in a small Texas town. As a dark-skinned child in an overwhelmingly white community, he learned the political implications of his "Indianness" earlier than most reservation-raised children, even though he had no

contact with Native American people or culture. It wasn't until he arrived in Santa Fe, a successful painter in his late thirties, that he grew curious about his Native American heritage. When GW first arrived in Santa Fe, he considered publicizing himself as an Indian artist. (At the time, his paintings consisted primarily of portraits of dogs and angels.) Once he became aware of the controversies over ethnic identity in the Native American art world, however, he decided against it, not wishing to incite the wrath of other Native artists or risk losing his status in the non-Indian art world. Nevertheless, he has started to search in earnest for his birth parents and has made several trips to the reservation town where he believes they were living when he was born.

11. Art as "contest," or subversive strategy, is the topic of a collection of essays edited by Jeremy MacClancy (1997). In his introduction, the editor explicates different indigenous art forms as creative challenges to the "colonial status quo" (8) in both the colonial and post-colonial eras.

Chapter 5

1. Similar critiques have been leveled at the colonial museums of European countries. For example, Annie E. Coombes views the turn-of-the-century British Museum as a veritable "temple of empire" (1994:109), where displays of magnificent African objects justified the imperialist project.

2. See especially the work of Fred Wilson (Corrin 1994).

3. According to James Stewart, curator and art history professor at the University of California, Berkeley, museum visitors spend an average of seven seconds looking at any one object or display.

4. Among the comments I frequently overheard in the NMAI galleries were, "I have one of those," and "That's like the one I saw at such-and-such a place, only nicer."

5. Parallel movements are occurring across the social sciences and humanities. For example, contributors to the seminal *Writing Culture: The Poetics and Politics of Ethnography* (Clifford and Marcus 1986) called for more "open" textual practices. As the anthropologist's representations are acknowledged to be partial and subjective, experimental writing techniques are engaged to more accurately describe the ways in which cultures are historically produced and actively contested (see epilogue).

6. According to Hilden and her co-authors, Native American consultants who were critical of Heye or his collecting methods were censored during the exhibit-planning stages (1995:53,60).

7. The most prominent case of state censorship in recent times occurred at the

Smithsonian Institution's National Air and Space Museum, when the exhibit questioning America's decision to bomb Japan during World War II was canceled in 1995.

8. For its 1995 exhibit "Living in Balance," the University of Pennsylvania Museum hired four Native American consultants—one each from the Navajo, Hopi, Zuni, and White Mountain Apache tribes—to advise curator Dorothy Washburn about the sacred and cultural connections these tribes have with their environments. As Washburn stated in her preface to the catalog, "[t]he exhibit does not celebrate the early explorers who excavated archaeological sites and sold the artifacts to the Museum, nor the early work by anthropologists, museum personnel, and other individuals who worked or traveled among the people of the Southwest" (1995:x). By focusing her exhibit on the spiritual, and thus the timeless, Washburn avoided the more sensitive intersection of collection and colonialism. If any political conflicts arose during her consultations with Native American experts, they were not mentioned in the catalog or the exhibit.

9. A significant exception to this pattern is the Museum at Warm Springs, in Warm Springs, Oregon, where several exhibits "bring the people into the present" (Dahl 1997:8).

Chapter 6

1. In the interest of brevity, and because the writing most accessible to me focused on the contemporary "fine arts" of painting and sculpture, at least two important genres of artistic production have been omitted from this chapter: contemporary pottery, textiles, and other works in so-called traditional media; and contemporary Inuit and Aleut prints and sculptures. These genres of work are written about in much the same way as the genres addressed here, but the criticism of works in traditional media can be less problematic when it does not have to address the issues of resistance and transculturalism.

2. On the link between art history and art criticism, see also Gee 1993.

3. Since this time the literature of Native American art history has been dominated by art historians, with the notable exception of anthropologist Nelson Graburn. Where arts are the topic of contemporary anthropological studies, they are generally contextualized and historicized (e.g., Parezo 1983). The similarity of this approach to that of the "new" art history suggests a rapprochement between the two disciplines.

4. In the years between 1941 and 1971, several comprehensive surveys of Native American art were published, including

Covarrubias 1954, Dockstader 1961, and Feder 1972. Northwest Coast art received increased critical attention, culminating in the seminal work of Bill Holm (1965). Because art historians relied on museum collections for their data, and because museum collections primarily consisted of historic material, most surveys neglected contemporary arts and artists. Anthropologists still writing about material culture were more attuned to contemporary developments, probably because their fieldwork brought them into contact with living artists. In John Adair's 1944 study of Navajo and Pueblo silversmiths, for example, the author devotes two chapters to the daily work of a "modern craftsman," the twenty-seven-year-old Tom Burnsides.

5. There are exceptions to this rule, especially among the enthusiastic female patrons of Southwestern arts. Anthropologist Clara Lee Tanner wrote about contemporary Southwestern painting (1957) as well as the work of contemporary Navajo weavers (1964). Dorothy Dunn (1955, 1968) documented the work of the young Native American painters she taught at the U.S. Indian School in Santa Fe. Both women, however, were products of their times, and

relied on romantic or primitivist stereotypes to validate contemporary Native American arts.

6. For a detailed account of the takeover of Alcatraz Island, see Fortunate Eagle 1992. For information on the American Indian Movement and the siege of Wounded Knee, see Smith and Warrior 1996.

7. Sixteen years later, three Native American artists were included in the New York Museum of Modern Art's 1988 survey, "Committed to Print: Social and Political Themes in Recent American Printed Art." According to curator Deborah Wye, the same pluralism that "extended [aesthetic approval] to art with discernable subject matter" (1988:8) in the late '60s and early '70s cleared space for the work of ethnic artists. Unfortunately, when Wye grouped prints by Jean LaMarr, Edgar Heap of Birds, and Rudy Begay in the section titled "Race/Culture," she inadvertently reinforced the racial framework that had excluded these works in the first place.

8. Soza split his time between activism and art, participating in the occupation of Alcatraz Island in 1970 and the takeover of the Bureau of Indian Affairs Building in Washington, D.C. in 1971. As he tells it, "I had various exhibits of my work from 1966 to 1973, but I was a federal fugitive at

the time, so I couldn't attend" (Soza in Rick Hill 1992:97).

9. As Charlotte Townsend-Gault wrote about contemporary First Nations art in Canada, "[g]iven the diversity of the work—in history and intent as well as appearance, native artists being confronted with as many aesthetic choices as any others—I would say that First Nations art is not an art category at all, but a shared socio-political situation, constituted by a devastating history, the powers of the Indian Act, the social geographies of the reservation system, by tribal and local politics, by the shifting demographics of the non-Native in pluralist society, and by the worldwide ethnic revival" (1995b:94, see also 1991:67).

10. The debate over the necessity of cultural context is significant, and I do not mean to imply that I have sided with one faction or the other. It is important to recognize, however, that this is no longer a battle between anthropologists and art historians. As the "new" art history shifts the scholarly gaze from objects to contexts of production, aesthetic judgment is losing favor in the art-historical discourse. In a sense, art history is becoming an anthropology of art, in method if not in result (see the essays in Marcus and Myers 1995, Phillips and Steiner 1999).

11. The issue of cultural relativism also complicates the situation. In a study that compared Anglo and Inuit evaluations of Inuit sculpture, Nelson Graburn found both a "remarkable lack of agreement among the White evaluators" and a "profound difference between the evaluations by White people and by the Inuit" (1986:271). Other anthropological studies of cross-cultural art appreciation support this finding (see the essays in Jopling 1971 and Forge 1973). But if Native American artists do evaluate their work differently from outsiders, it is not clear how this fact should influence the criticism of a body of work collected primarily by outsiders.

12. According to Bigfeather, at least one artist wrote a letter to the editor protesting Zimmer's insensitive review.

Chapter 7

1. In the historical study *Imagining Indians in the Southwest: Persistent Visions of a Primitive Past*, Dilworth invokes collecting as a metaphor for the representation of Native Americans. Collecting is also considered a representational strategy "implicit in the process[es] of writing, painting, photographing, and sightseeing" (Dilworth 1996:7).

2. One of the few collectors who expressed

disinterest in meeting tribal people said he preferred to experience Indian country in the comfort of his living room, where he could read Tony Hillerman novels and thumb through the pages of *American Indian Art* magazine. But even this man occasionally attended pow-wows, where he would sit alone in the bleachers and watch from a distance.

3. A few studies have investigated Native American stereotypes of non-Indians (Basso 1979, Holden 1976), but on the whole, as anthropologist Deirdre Evans-Pritchard (1989) points out, this is a much-neglected field.

4. For a related discussion of the problems of translating Native American literature, see Krupat 1992.

5. In the 1920s, Atchison, Topeka & Santa Fe Railway joined the Fred Harvey company in launching "Indian Detours," which offered chauffeured, guided automobile excursions into the wilderness of Arizona's "Indian Country." In her analysis of this venture, anthropologist Marta Weigle called it "engineering ethnic tourism" (1989:133). Today, tribes have more control over tourism on their land and are engineering their own "detours."

6. Lujan cited her "unique access to the daily life of the pueblo due to her relationships within the pueblo and her American Indian identity" (1993:107) as an advantage for researching the effects of tourism in Taos.

7. Lujan estimated the annual revenue from tourism in 1993 to be $250,000.

8. Other Pueblos are more restrictive in their attitudes toward tourists. In Santa Domingo, for instance, tourism in residential areas is not allowed, and non-tribal members are required to leave the area before sundown. Taos's permissive attitude toward tourism, and its dependence on tourist dollars, are frequently criticized by members of more conservative Pueblos. Lujan defends her community's actions by emphasizing that "[t]he traditional culture does not appear to be eroding any more quickly at Taos than at other pueblos that do not admit tourists" (1993:118).

9. Zuni Pueblo has irregularly enforced a similar policy of closing its main street during the annual Shalako ceremony. This angers merchants, especially art dealers, who earn the majority of their annual revenue during this three-day holiday weekend.

10. Brody also characterized Allan Houser's *Apache Girls' Puberty Rite* (1938) as "social commentary," due to its realistic depiction of the "grimmer aspects of reservation

life—the medicine man's posture is slumped, defeated; the girls wear traditional costume, but everyone else wears patched White-man's clothing" (Brody 1971:146). But because Houser's painting otherwise adhered to the decorative ideals of the Santa Fe Studio School, "the result was a picture so subtle as to be almost innocuous and certainly ambivalent" (164).

11. The fact that a merely realistic portrayal of Indian-white relations can categorize an artwork as "political" is a sad reflection on the degree to which patrons have denied colonial power relations.

Works cited

Abbott, Lawrence. 1994. "Spaces for Artistic Possibility: An Interview With Gerald McMaster." *Akwe:kon Journal* 11(1):2–15.

Abeyta, Tony. 1996. Conversation with author. Taos, N.Mex., 23 July.

Adair, John. 1944. *The Navajo and Pueblo Silversmiths.* Norman: University of Oklahoma Press.

Allison, Lesli. 1991. "The Hazy Borderland Between Worlds." *Pasatiempo* (16–22 August):14.

Alsop, Joseph. 1982. *The Rare Art Traditions.* New York: Harper and Row.

American Indian Art. 1995. "Museum Acquisitions." 20(4):94.

———. 1997. "Museum Acquisitions." 22(3):104.

Ames, Michael M. 1992. *Cannibal Tours and Glass Boxes: The Anthropology of Museums.* Vancouver: University of British Colombia Press.

Anderson, Benedict. 1983. *Imagined Communities: Reflections on the Origin and Spread of Nationalism.* London: Verso.

Archuleta, Margaret. 1988. "Networking: From Sacramento to Seattle." *Native Peoples* 1(3):19–23.

Archuleta, Margaret and Rennard Strickland. 1991. *Shared Visions: Native American Painters and Sculptors in the Twentieth Century.* New York: New Press.

Arieff, Allison. 1995. "A Different Sort of (P)reservation: Some Thoughts on the National Museum of the American Indian." *Museum Anthropology* 19(2):78–90.

Art Guide. 1988. "Cross Culture." 21.

Ashton, Dore. 1982. *American Art Since 1945.* New York: Oxford University Press.

Baer, Joshua. 1996. "Interview with Guy Cross." *THE Magazine* (August):48–49.

Basso, Keith. 1979. *Portraits of "The Whiteman": Linguistic Play and Cultural Symbols Among the Western Apache.* Cambridge, England: Cambridge University Press.

Bear Claw, Dean Curtis. 1995. Conversation with author. New York, N.Y., 6 July.

Becker, Howard S. 1982. *Art Worlds.* Berkeley: University of California Press.

Belting, Hans. 1987. *The End of the History of Art?* Translated by Christopher Wood. Chicago: University of Chicago Press.

Benjamin, Walter. 1968. "The Work of Art in the Age of Mechanical Reproduction." Pp. 219–53 in *Illuminations,* edited by Hannah Arendt. Translated by Harry Zohn. New York: Harcourt, Brace and World.

Bensley, Lis. 1993. "Women Share a Vision, Sense of Culture." *Pasatiempo* (26 August).

Berkhofer, Robert F. 1979. *The White Man's Indian: Images of the American Indian from Columbus to the Present.* New York: Vintage Books.

Berlo, Janet Catherine, ed. 1992. *The Early Years of Native American Art History.* Seattle: University of Washington Press.

Berlo, Janet Catherine and Ruth Phillips. 1992. "Vitalizing Things of the Past: Museum Representations of Native North American Art in the 1990s." *Museum Anthropology* 16(1):29–43.

Bernstein, Bruce. 1988. *Frank LaPena: The World is a Gift.* Santa Fe: Wheelwright Museum.

Bernstein, Bruce, ed. 1994. "Southwestern Native Fairs and Markets." *Expedition* 36(1).

Bhabha, Homi K. 1993. "Beyond the Pale: Art in the Age of Multicultural Translation." Pp. 62–73 in *1993 Biennial Exhibition,* edited by Elizabeth Sussman. New York: Whitney Museum of American Art.

Bigfeather, Joanna Osburn. 1995. Essay. Pp. 4–6 in *Legacies: Contemporary Art by Native American Women: September 3–October 29,* Castle Gallery, College of New Rochelle, N.Y.

Boas, Franz. 1955 [1927]. *Primitive Art.* New York: Dover Publications.

Bordewich, Fergus M. 1996. "Revolution in Indian Country." *American Heritage* 47(4):34–46.

Bourdieu, Pierre. 1971. "Intellectual Field and Creative Project." Pp. 161–88 in *Knowledge and Control: New Directions for the Sociology of Education*, edited by Michael Young. London: Collier-Macmillan.

———. 1984. *Distinction: A Social Critique of the Judgement of Taste.* Cambridge, Mass.: Harvard University Press.

Brody, J. J. 1971. *Indian Painters and White Patrons.* Albuquerque: University of New Mexico Press.

———. 1997. "Contextualizing Native American Art History: A Dialogue Between Anthropologists, Art Historians, and Native American Artists." Presented at symposium, "Memory and Imagination in Twentieth-Century Native American Indian Art" at Oakland Museum of California.

Brooke, James. 1997. "Sales of Indian Crafts Boom and So Do Fakes." *New York Times* (2 August):A6.

Browne, Rita-Jean and Mary Lee Nolan. 1980. "Western Indian Reservation Tourism Development." *Annals of Tourism Research* 16:360–76.

Butterfield and Butterfield (Auctioneers and Appraisers, San Francisco). 1996. *Native American, Pre-Columbian, African, Oceanic and Other Tribal Works of Art* (10 December).

Carpenter, Edmund. 1972. *Oh, What a Blow that Phantom Gave Me!* New York: Holt, Rinehart and Winston.

———. 1991. "Repatriation Policy and the Heye Collection." *Museum Anthropology* 15(3):15–18.

Castile, George Pierre. 1996. "The Commodification of Indian Identity." *American Anthropologist* 98(4):743–49

Christie's (New York). 1995. *Important Modern Works of Art from the Collection of Mr. and Mrs. Ralph F. Colin* (10 May).

Churchill, Ward. 1992. "Nobody's Pet Poodle." *Z Magazine* 5(2):68–72.

Clark, Janet E. 1994. "To Exhibit, Interpret, and Collect: A Short History of Collecting and Exhibiting Contemporary Native Art at the Thunder Bay Art Gallery." Pp. 4–6 in *Thunder Bay Art Gallery Mandate Study.* Thunder Bay, Ontario: Thunder Bay Art Gallery.

Clifford, James. 1988. *The Predicament of Culture: Twentieth-Century Ethnography, Literature, and Art.* Cambridge, Mass.: Harvard University Press.

———. 1989. "The Global Issue: A Symposium." *Art in America* 77(7):86–87, 152–53.

———. 1991. "Four Northwest Coast Museums: Travel Reflections." Pp. 212–54 in *Exhibiting Cultures,* edited by Ivan Karp and Steven Lavine. Washington, D.C.: Smithsonian Institution Press.

Clifford, James and George E. Marcus, eds. 1986. *Writing Culture: The Poetics and Politics of Ethnography.* Berkeley: University of California Press.

Coe, Ralph T. 1986. *Lost and Found Traditions: Native*

American Art 1965–1985. Seattle: University of
Washington Press.

———. 1995. "The Eugene and Clare Thaw Collection
of American Indian Art: The Making of a Collection."
Heritage 11(4): 6–19.

Cohodas, Marvin. 1992. "Louisa Keyser and the Cohns:
Mythmaking and Basket Making in the American
West." Pp. 88–133 in *The Early Years of Native American
Art History,* edited by Janet Catherine Berlo. Seattle:
University of Washington Press.

Cole, Douglas. 1985. *Captured Heritage: The Scramble
for Northwest Coast Artifacts.* Seattle: University of
Washington Press.

Coombes, Annie E. 1994. *Reinventing Africa: Museums,
Material Culture and Popular Imagination.* New Haven,
Conn.: Yale University Press.

Cooper, James Fenimore. 1980 [1827]. *The Prairie.* New
York: New American Library.

Corrin, Lisa, ed. 1994. *Mining the Museum: An Installation
by Fred Wilson.* New York: New Press.

Corrow, Richard N. 1996. "Sell A Mask—Or Basket,
And Go To Jail?" *ATADA Newsletter* 7(1):6–7.

Cotter, Holland. 1994. "New Museum Celebrating
American Indian Voices." *New York Times* (28
October):C1, C14.

Covarrubias, Miguel. 1954. *The Eagle, the Jaguar, and the
Serpent: Indian Art of the Americas.* New York: Alfred A.
Knopf.

Dahl, Kathleen A. 1997. "Public Images: Native
Presentations of History and Identity." Unpublished
manuscript.

Deitch, Lewis I. 1989. "The Impact of Tourism on the
Arts and Crafts of the Indians of the Southwestern
United States." Pp. 223–35 in *Hosts and Guests: The
Anthropology of Tourism,* edited by Valene L. Smith.
Philadelphia: University of Pennsylvania Press.

Deloria, Vine, Jr. 1988 [1969]. *Custer Died For Your
Sins: An Indian Manifesto.* Norman: University of
Oklahoma Press.

Dilworth, Leah. 1996. *Imagining Indians in the Southwest:*
Persistent Visions of a Primitive Past. Washington, D.C.:
Smithsonian Institution Press.

Dobkins, Rebecca. 1995. "From Vanishing to Visible:
Maidu Indian Arts and the Uses of Tradition." Ph.D.
diss., University of California, Berkeley.

Dockstader, Frederick J. 1961. *Indian Art in America:
The Arts and Crafts of the North American Indian.*
Greenwich, Conn.: New York Graphic Society.

Dominguez, Virginia. 1987. "Of Other Peoples:
Beyond the Salvage Paradigm." Pp. 131–37 in
Discussions in Contemporary Culture, edited by Hal
Foster. Seattle: Bay Press.

Douglas, Frederic H. and Rene d'Harnoncourt. 1948
[1941]. *Indian Art of the United States.* New York:
Museum of Modern Art.

Dozier, Deborah S. 1992. Review of "Objects of Myth
and Memory: American Indian Art at the Brooklyn
Museum." *American Indian Culture and Research
Journal* 16(2):240–42.

Dubin, Margaret. 1995. "The Artist as Community
Healer: Atlatl Biennial Conference." *Native Peoples*
8(2):48–49.

———. 1998. "Joanna Osburn Bigfeather." In *St. James
Guide to Native North American Artists,* edited by
Roger Matuz. Detroit: St. James Press.

Duffek, Karen. 1989. "Lyle Wilson: When Worlds
Collide." University of British Columbia Museum of
Anthropology Museum, note no. 28.

Dunn, Dorothy. 1955. "America's First Painters." *National
Geographic Magazine* 57(3):349–78.

———. 1968. *American Indian Painting of the Southwest
and Plains Areas.* Albuquerque: University of New
Mexico Press.

Durham, Jimmie. 1992. "Cowboys and . . . Notes on Art,
Literature, and American Indians in the Modern
American Mind." Pp. 423–38 in *The State of Native
America: Genocide, Colonization, and Resistance,* edited
by M. Annette Jaimes. Boston: South End Press.

Economist. 1995. "The Indians Lose Again."
(28 January):81–82.

Eddington, Patrick and Susan Makov. 1995. *Trading Post Guidebook: Where to Find the Trading Posts, Galleries, Auctions, Artists, and Museums of the Four Corners Region.* Flagstaff, Ariz.: Northland Publishing.

Errington, Shelly. 1998. *The Death of the Authentic Primitive and Other Tales of Progress.* Berkeley: University of California Press.

Evans-Pritchard, Deirdre. 1989. "How 'They' See 'Us': Native American Images of Tourists." *Annals of Tourism Research* 16:89–105.

Fabian, Johannes. 1983. *Time and the Other: How Anthropology Makes Its Object.* New York: Columbia University Press.

Fane, Diane. 1991. "The Language of Things: Stewart Culin as Collector." Pp. 13–27 in *Objects of Myth and Memory: American Indian Art at the Brooklyn Museum,* edited by Diane Fane, Ira Jacknis, and Lise Breen. Brooklyn: Brooklyn Museum in association with University of Washington Press.

Feder, Norman. 1972. *Two Hundred Years of North American Indian Art.* New York: Praeger.

Farnsworth, Clyde H. 1997. "Two Exposed Artists, Neither Aboriginal (Nor Original) After All." *New York Times* (2 April):B1, B11.

Ferguson, T. J. and Wilfred Eriacho. 1990. "*Ahayu:Da* Zuni War Gods." *Native Peoples* 4(1):6–12.

Fienup-Riordan, Ann. 1996. *The Living Tradition of Yup'ik Masks.* Seattle: University of Washington Press.

Force, Lisa. 1993. "Indian Arts Law . . . Harm or Help?" *Art-Talk* (August/September):22–23.

Forge, Anthony, ed. 1973. *Primitive Art and Society.* London: Oxford University Press.

Fortunate Eagle, Adam. 1992. *Alcatraz! Alcatraz! The Indian Occupation of 1969–1971.* Berkeley: Heyday Books.

Francis, Daniel. 1992. *The Imaginary Indian: The Image of the Indian in Canadian Culture.* Vancouver: Arsenal Pulp Press.

Freund, Thatcher. 1993. *Objects of Desire: The Lives of Antiques and Those Who Pursue Them.* New York: Pantheon Books.

Frisbie, Charlotte J. 1987. *Navajo Medicine Bundles or Jish: Acquisition, Transmission, and Disposition in the Past and Present.* Albuquerque: University of New Mexico Press.

Gamerman, Amy. 1992. "Indian Museum Takes Shelter in Beaux-Arts Wickiup." *Wall Street Journal* (17 November):A14.

Garmhausen, Winona. 1988. *The History of Indian Arts Education in Santa Fe.* Santa Fe: Sunstone Press.

Gee, Malcolm, ed. 1993. *Art Criticism Since 1900.* Manchester, England: Manchester University Press.

Giago, Tim. 1991. "Welcome to the Museum of American Stereotypes." *Indian Country Today* (21 September).

Gill, Sam D. 1987. *Mother Earth: An American Story.* Chicago: University of Chicago Press.

Gordon, Beverly. 1988. "American Indian Art: The Collecting Experience." Elvehjem Museum of Art, University of Wisconsin–Madison, 7 May–3 July, 1988. Madison: Regents of University of Wisconsin.

Gouveia, Georgette. 1995. "Current Exhibit at CNR is Both Beautiful and Bitter." *Gannett Suburban Newspapers* (Westchester County, N.Y.) (17 September):5C.

Graburn, Nelson. 1977. "The Museum and Visitor Experience." Pp. 131–37 in *The Visitor and the Museum,* edited by Linda Draperu. Seattle: American Association of Museums.

———. 1986. "White Evaluation of the Quality of Inuit Sculpture." *Etudes/Inuit/Studies* 10(1–2):271–83.

Graburn, Nelson H. H., ed. 1976. *Ethnic and Tourist Arts: Cultural Expressions from the Fourth World.* Berkeley: University of California Press.

Graburn, Nelson and Molly Lee. 1996. "Does a Collection Represent a Culture? The Alaska Commercial Company Collection." Unpublished manuscript.

Greenberg, Clement. 1993 [1961]. "The Identity of Art." Pp. 131–37 in *Clement Greenberg: The Collected Essays and Criticism,* edited by John O'Brianu. Chicago: University of Chicago Press.

Gritton, Joy L. 1991. "The Institute of American Indian Arts: A Convergence of Ideologies." Pp. 131–37 in *Shared Visions: Native American Painters and Sculptors in the Twentieth Century,* edited by Margaret Archuleta and Rennard Strickland. New York: New Press.

———. 1992. "Cross-Cultural Education vs. Modernist Imperialism: The Institute of American Indian Arts." *Art Journal* 51(3):28–35.

———. 2000. *The Institute of American Indian Arts: Modernism and U.S. Indian Policy.* Albuquerque: University of New Mexico Press.

Gupta, Akhil and James Ferguson, eds. 1997a. *Anthropological Locations: Boundaries and Grounds of a Field Science.* Berkeley: University of California Press.

———. 1997b. *Culture, Power, Place: Explorations in Critical Anthropology.* Durham, N.C.: Duke University Press.

Halle, David. 1993a. "The Audience for 'Primitive' Art in Houses in the New York Region." *The Art Bulletin* 75(3):397–414.

———. 1993b. *Inside Culture: Art and Class in the American Home.* Chicago: University of Chicago Press.

Harjo, Suzan. 1991. "Legislation Stiffens Art Authenticity Laws." *Crosswinds* (August).

Hart, William. 1987. "Indian Artists Claim Fakes Hurting Sales." *The Arizona Republic* (6 September):E3.

Helms, Mary W. 1994. "Essay on Objects: Interpretations of Distance Made Tangible." Pp. 355–77 in *Implicit Understandings: Observing, Reporting, and Reflecting on the Encounters Between Europeans and Other Peoples in the Early Modern Era,* edited by Stuart B. Schwartz. Cambridge, England: Cambridge University Press.

Hilden, Patricia Penn, Shari Huhndorf, and Carol Kalafatic. 1995. "Fry Bread and Wild West Shows: The 'New' National Museum of the American Indian." Unpublished manuscript.

Hill, R. William. 1997. "Marilyn Monroe He Ain't: Pop Artist Meets Pop Activist." *Aboriginal Voices* 4(2):49.

Hill, Rick. 1992. *Creativity is Our Tradition: Three Decades of Contemporary Indian Art at the Institute of American Indian Arts.* Santa Fe: Institute of American Indian and Alaska Native Culture and Arts Development.

Hill, Tom and Richard W. Hill Sr., eds. 1994. *Creation's Journey: Native American Identity and Belief.* Washington, D.C.: Smithsonian Institution Press.

Hinsley, Curtis M. 1981. *The Smithsonian and the American Indian.* Washington, D.C.: Smithsonian Institution Press.

Hobsbawm, Eric J. 1983 "Introduction: Inventing Traditions." Pp. 1–14 in *The Invention of Tradition,* edited by Eric J. Hobsbawm and Terence Ranger. Cambridge, England: Cambridge University Press.

Hoffman, Gerhard. 1987. "Frames of Reference: Native American Art in the Context of Modern and Postmodern Art." *ArtSpace* 11(2):24–30.

Holden, Madronna. 1976. "'Making All the Crooked Ways Straight': The Satirical Portrait of Whites in Coast Salish Folklore.: *Journal of American Folklore Quarterly* (winter):144–61.

Holm, Bill. 1965. *Northwest Coast Indian Art: An Analysis of Form.* Seattle: University of Washington Press.

Holmes, Sue. 1985. "Buyers Beware: Fakes Flood Indian Market." *Phoenix Gazette* (8 April).

Horner, Alice E. 1990. "The Assumption of Tradition: Creating, Collecting, and Conserving Cultural Artifacts in the Cameroon Grassfields." Ph.D. diss., University of California, Berkeley.

Hoving, Thomas. 1996. *False Impressions: The Hunt for Big-Time Art Fakes.* New York: Simon and Schuster.

Howard, Kathleen L. and Diana F. Pardue. 1996. *Inventing the Southwest: The Fred Harvey Company and Native American Art.* Flagstaff, Ariz.: Northland Press.

Indian Arts and Crafts Association. 1994. *Directory of Members and Buyers Guide.* Albuquerque, N.Mex.

Isaacs, Jennifer. 1992. *Aboriginality: Contemporary Aboriginal Paintings and Prints.* Queensland, Australia: University of Queensland Press.

Jacknis, Ira. 1995. Presentation at panel discussion, "Is it the Real Thing? Art, Artifact, Authenticity." Phoebe Hearst Museum of Anthropology, University of California, Berkeley.

Johnson, Thomas. 1997. "Native American Enrollment and Identity." *Anthropology Newsletter* 38(3):19–20.

Johnston, Susanna and Tim Beddow. 1986. *Collecting: The Passionate Pastime.* New York: Harper and Row.

Jopling, Carol F., ed. 1971. *Art and Aesthetics in Primitive Societies.* New York: E. P. Dutton and Company.

King, J. C. H. 1981. *Artificial Curiosities from the Northwest Coast of America.* London: British Museum Publications, Ltd.

Kotik, Charlotta. 1994. "The Legacy of Signs: Reflections on Adolph Gottlieb's Pictographs." Pp. 59-67 in *The Pictographs of Adolph Gottlieb,* edited by Lawrence Alloway, et al. New York: Hudson Hills Press in association with the Adolph and Esther Gottlieb Foundation, Inc.

Krantz, Claire Wolfe. 1989. "Interview: Bob Haozous." *Art Papers* (March/April):23–26.

Krupat, Arnold. 1992. *Ethnocriticism: Ethnography, History, Literature.* Berkeley: University of California Press.

Lanford, Benson. 1994. "The History of Collecting American Indian Art: The Beginnings to the Early Nineteenth Century." *Tribal Arts* 1(4):58–66.

———. 1995. "The History of Collecting American Indian Art, Part Two: The Nineteenth and Twentieth Centuries." *Tribal Arts* 2(1):62–71.

LaPena, Frank. 1997. Conversation with author. Oakland, Calif., 19 April.

———. 1997. "What Is Tradition?" Presented at symposium, "Memory and Imagination in Twentieth-Century Native American Indian Art," at Oakland Museum of California.

Laxson, Joan D. 1991. "How 'We' See 'Them': Tourism and Native Americans." *Annals of Tourism Research* 18:365–91.

Lee, Molly. 1991. "Appropriating the Primitive: Turn-of-the-Century Collection and Display of Native Alaskan Art." *Arctic Anthropology* 23(1):6–15.

Lemann, Nicholas. 1987. "Fake Masks." *The Atlantic* 260(5):24–38.

Lévi-Strauss, Claude. 1982. *The Way of the Masks.* Translated by Sylvia Modelski. Seattle: University of Washington Press.

Linn, Natalie Fay. 1990. "In Search of the Natural: American Indian Basketry and the Arts and Crafts Movement." *Antiques and Fine Art* 8(1):126–31.

Linsley, Robert. 1995. "Yuxweluptun and the West Coast Landscape." Pp. 23–32 in *Lawrence Paul Yuxweluptun: Born to Live and Die on Your Colonialist Reservations,* edited by Charlotte Townsend-Gault, Scott Watson, and Lawrence Paul Yuxweluptun. Vancouver: University of British Columbia.

Lippard, Lucy R. 1990. *Mixed Blessings: New Art in a Multicultural America.* New York: Pantheon Books.

———. 1993. "Jimmie Durham: Postmodernist 'Savage.'" *Art in America* 81(2):62–69.

Lomahaftewa, Dan. 1996. Conversation with author. Santa Fe, N.Mex., 17 July.

Lomawaima, K. Tsianina. 1994. *They Called it Prairie Light.* Lincoln: University of Nebraska Press.

Lujan, Carol Chiago. 1993. "A Sociological View of Tourism in an American Indian Community: Maintaining Cultural Integrity at Taos Pueblo." *American Indian Culture and Research Journal* 17(3):101–20.

MacCannell, Dean. 1989 [1976]. *The Tourist: A New Theory of the Leisure Class.* New York: Schocken Books.

MacClancy, Jeremy, ed. 1997. *Contesting Art: Art, Politics, and Identity in the Modern World.* Oxford: Berg.

Malinowski, Bronislaw. 1953 [1922]. *Argonauts of the Western Pacific.* New York: E. P. Dutton and Company.

Marcus, George E. and Michael M. J. Fischer. 1986. *Anthropology as Cultural Critique: An Experimental Moment in the Human Sciences.* Chicago: University of Chicago Press.

Marcus, George E. and Fred R. Myers, eds. 1995. *The Traffic in Culture: Refiguring Art and Anthropology.* Berkeley: University of California Press.

Masayesva, Victor. 1994. "Through Native Eyes: The Emerging Native American Aesthetic." *The Independent* 17(10):20–21, 27.

Masco, Joseph. 1996. "Competitive Displays: Negotiating Genealogical Rights to the Potlatch at the American Museum of Natural History." *American Anthropologist* 98(4):837–52.

McCoy, Mary. 1992. "'Submoloc': Reversing the Tide." *Washington Post* (27 June).

McGreevy, Susan Brown. 1993. Review of "Reflections of the Weaver's World: The Gloria F. Ross Collection of Contemporary Navajo Weaving." *American Indian Culture and Research Journal* 17(2):225–28.

McMaster, Gerald R. 1995. "Borderzones: The 'Injunuity' of Aesthetic Tricks." *Cultural Studies* 9(1):74–90.

Menchaca, Martha. 1993. "Chicano Indianism: A Historical Account of Racial Repression in the United States." *American Ethnologist* 20(3):583–603.

Mills, Jeanette C. 1989. "The Meares Island Controversy and Joe David: Art in Support of a Cause." *American Indian Art* 14(4):60–69.

Minor, Vernon Hyde. 1994. *Art History's History.* Englewood Cliffs, N.J.: Prentice Hall, Inc.

Mitchell, Nancy Marie. 1993. "The Negotiated Role of Contemporary American Indian Artists: A Study in Marginality." Ph.D. diss., Stanford University.

Mithlo, Nancy Marie. 1995. "Is There Really No Word For Art in Our Language?" Presented at the meeting of the Native American Art Studies Association in Tulsa, Okla.

Mullin, Molly. 1992. "The Patronage of Difference: Making Indian Art 'Art, Not Ethnology.'" *Cultural Anthropology* 7(4):395–424.

Myers, Fred R. 1989. "Truth, Beauty, and Pintupi Painting." *Visual Anthropology* 2:163–95.

———. 1991. "Representing Culture: The Production of Discourse(s) for Aboriginal Acrylic Paintings." *Cultural Anthropology* 6(1):26–62.

———. 1994. "Culture-Making: Performing Aboriginality at the Asia Society Gallery." *American Ethnologist* 21(4):679–99.

Nabokov, Peter. 1988. "Cultivating Themselves: The Inter-play of Crow Indian Religion and History." Ph.D. diss., University of California, Berkeley.

Nader, Laura. 1972. "Up the Anthropologist: Perspectives Gained from Studying Up." Pp. 285–311 in *Reinventing Anthropology,* edited by Dell Hymes. New York: Pantheon Press.

New York Times. 1993. "Museum Set to Lose Indian Treasure" (19 February):A12.

Norick, Frank. 1995. Conversation with author. Berkeley, Calif., 6 April.

Ostrow, Saul. 1994. "Clement Greenberg: The Last Interview." *World Art* (November):24–32.

Oxendine, Lloyd E. 1972. "23 Contemporary Indian Artists." *Art in America* 60(4):58–69.

Parezo, Nancy. 1983. *Navajo Sandpainting: From Religious Act to Commercial Art.* Tucson: University of Arizona Press.

———. 1990. "A Multitude of Markets." *Journal of the Southwest* 32(4):563–75.

Parsons, Elsie Clews. 1962. "Isleta Paintings." In *Bureau of American Ethnology Bulletin* 181. Washington, D.C.: Smithsonian Institution Press.

Patton, Phil. 1995. "Today's Crafts Join Our Nation's Past at the White House." *Smithsonian* 26(3):52–57.

Pearce, Roy Harvey. 1988 [1953]. *Savagism and Civilization: A Study of the Indian and the American Mind.* Berkeley: University of California Press.

Penney, David W. 1995. "The Poetics of Museum Representations: Tropes of Recent American Indian Art Exhibitions." Presented at symposium, "The Changing Presentation of the American Indian" at the National Museum of the American Indian, New York.

Peterson, William. 1990. "Emmi Whitehorse." *ArtSpace* (July/August):38–39.

Pevar, Stephen L. 1992. *The Rights of Indians and Tribes.* Carbondale: Southern Illinois University Press.

Phillips, Ruth B. 1995a. "Why Not Tourist Art? Significant Silences in Native American Museum Representations." Pp. 4–6 in *After Colonialism: Imperial Histories and Postcolonial Displacements,* edited by Gyan Prakash. Princeton, N.J.: Princeton University Press.

———. 1995b. "Great Lakes Birchbark Souvenir Art in the Victorian Period." Presented at conference, "Symposium on American Indian Art," at the meeting of the New York State Historical Association, Cooperstown, N.Y.

Phillips, Ruth B. and Christopher B. Steiner, eds. 1999. *Unpacking Culture: Art and Commodity in Colonial and Postcolonial Worlds.* Berkeley: University of California Press.

Rees, A. L. and Frances Borzello, eds. 1988. *The New Art History.* Atlantic Highlands, N.J.: Humanities Press.

Reichard, Gladys A. 1928. *Social Life of the Navajo Indians: With Some Attention to Minor Ceremonies.* New York: Columbia University Press.

Riding, Alan. 1995. "Taking African Creativity Onto Europe's Cultural Stage." *New York Times* (4 October):C13.

Rosenak, Chuck and Jan Rosenak. 1994. *The People Speak: Navajo Folk Art.* Flagstaff, Ariz.: Northland Publishers.

Rushing, W. Jackson. 1992a. "Marketing the Affinity of the Primitive and the Modern." Pp. 191–236 in *The Early Years of Native American Art History,* edited by Janet Berlo. Seattle: University of Washington Press.

———. 1992b. "Critical Issues in Recent Native American Art." *Art Journal* 51(3):6–14.

———. 1994a. "Contemporary Native American Art: A Critical Perspective From the United States." Pp. 28–33 in *Thunder Bay Art Gallery Mandate Study.* Thunder Bay, Ontario: Thunder Bay Art Gallery.

———. 1994b. "Doug Coffin's 'Many Moons.'" *Akwe:kon Journal* 11(1):30–31.

———. 1995. *Native American Art and the New York Avant-Garde: A History of Cultural Primitivism.* Austin: University of Texas Press.

———. 1997. Telephone conversation with author, 17 June.

Russell, George. 1992. *The American Indian Digest.* Phoenix: Thunderbird Enterprises.

Ryan, Allan J. 1995. "The Trickster Shift: A New Paradigm in Contemporary Canadian Native Art." Ph.D. diss., University of British Columbia.

Sanborn, Andrea. 1995. "Perceptions and Misconceptions." *U'mista Cultural Society Newsletter* (28 April).

Sandlin, Scott. 1996. "Artifact Seller Convicted: Jury Finds Objects Are Navajo Legacy." ATADA Newsletter 7(1):4–5. (Reprinted from *Albuquerque Journal.*)

Sasser, Elizabeth S. 1983. "A Room With a View." *Southwest Art* 13(7):86–91.

Schneider, Arnd. 1996. "Uneasy Relationships: Contemporary Artists and Anthropology." *Journal of Material Culture* 1(2):183–210.

Schrader, Robert F. 1983. *The Indian Arts and Crafts Board.* Albuquerque: University of New Mexico Press.

Shaffer, Mark and Bill Donovan. 1994. "Fake Kachinas Offend Hopis." *Arizona Republic* (30 January):A1, A11.

Sheffield, Gail K. 1997. *The Arbitrary Indian: The Indian Arts and Crafts Act of 1990.* Norman: University of Oklahoma Press.

Shepard, Sam. 1973. "Left Handed Kachina." In *Hawk Moon.* New York: Performing Arts Journal Publications.

Simmons, William S. 1981. "Cultural Bias in the New England Puritans' Perception of Indians." *William and Mary Quarterly* 38:55–72.

Smith, Paul Chaat and Robert Allen Warrior. 1996. *Like A Hurricane: The Indian Movement from Alcatraz to Wounded Knee.* New York: New Press.

Snyder, George. 1993. "Zuni Fetishes Are More Than Art." *San Francisco Chronicle* (23 July):A1, A4.

Southwest Planning and Marketing. 1996. "Institute of American Indian Arts: Impact Assessment and Market Study." Santa Fe: Institute of American Indian Arts.

Spinden, Herbert J. 1931. "Fine Art and the First Americans." Pp. 3–8 in *Introduction to American Indian Art, Part Two.* New York: The Exposition of Indian Tribal Arts.

Sprengelmeyer, M. E. 1993. "Who's An Indian Artist and Who's Not?" *Santa Fe Reporter* (14–20 April).

Steiner, Christopher B. 1994. *African Art in Transit.* Cambridge, England: Cambridge University Press.

———. 1995. Presentation at panel discussion, "Is it the Real Thing? Art, Artifact, Authenticity." Phoebe Hearst Museum of Anthropology, University of California, Berkeley.

Stewart, Susan. 1993. *On Longing: Narratives of the Miniature, the Gigantic, the Souvenir, the Collection.* Durham, N.C.: Duke University Press.

Strickland, Rennard. 1986. "Tall Visitor at the Indian Gallery; or, The Future of Native American Art." Pp. 283–306 in *The Arts of the North American Indian: Native Traditions in Evolution,* edited by Edwin Wade. New York: Hudson Hills Press.

———. 1994. *Sharing the Heritage: American Indian Art from Oklahoma Private Collections.* Norman: Fred Jones, Jr. Museum of Art, University of Oklahoma.

Sweet, Jill D. 1991. "'Let 'Em Loose': Pueblo Indian Management of Tourism." *American Indian Culture and Research Journal* 15(4):59–74.

Tanner, Clara Lee. 1957. *Southwest Indian Painting.* Tucson: University of Arizona Press.

———. 1960. "The Influence of The White Man on Southwest Indian Art." *Ethnohistory* 7(2):137–50.

———. 1964. "Modern Navajo Weaving." *Arizona Highways* 60(9):6–20.

Teters, Charlene. 1997. "Jan Cicero Gallery." *Indian Artist* 3(1):36.

Torgovnick, Marianna. 1990. *Gone Primitive: Savage Intellects, Modern Lives.* Chicago: University of Chicago Press.

Townsend-Gault, Charlotte. 1991. "Having Voices and Using Them: First Nations Artists and Native 'Art.'" *Artsmagazine* 65(6):65–70.

———. 1995a. "The Salvation Art of Yuxweluptun." Pp. 7–28 in *Lawrence Paul Yuxweluptun: Born to Live and Die on Your Colonialist Reservations,* edited by Charlotte Townsend-Gault, Scott Watson, and Lawrence Paul Yuxweluptun. Vancouver: University of British Columbia Press.

———. 1995b. "Translation or Perversion?: Showing First Nations Art in Canada." *Cultural Studies* 9(1):91–105.

———. 1998. "Yuxweluptun." Pp. 643–44 in *St. James Guide to Native North American Artists,* edited by Roger Matuz. Detroit: St. James Press.

Traugott, Joseph. 1992. "Native American Artists and the Postmodern Cultural Divide." *Art Journal* 51(3):36–43.

U.S. House. 1990. *Report 101–400, Part 1: Expanding the Powers of the Indian Arts and Crafts Board, and for Other Purposes.* 101st Cong., 2d session, H.R. 2006.

Varnedoe, Kirk. 1984. "Abstract Expressionism." Pp. 615–60 in *Primitivism in Twentieth Century Art,* edited by William Rubin. New York: Museum of Modern Art.

Vincent, Gilbert. 1995. "The Eugene and Clare Thaw Collection of American Indian Art." *Antiques* 148(1):62–69.

Vizenor, Gerald. 1994. *Manifest Manners: Postindian Warriors of Survivance.* Hanover, N.H.: University Press of New England.

———. 1995a. "Ishi and the Wood Ducks." Pp. 299–336 in *Native American Literature: A Brief Introduction and Anthology,* edited by Gerald Vizenor. New York: Harper Collins College Publishers.

Vizenor, Gerald, ed. 1995b. *Native American Literature: A Brief Introduction and Anthology.* New York: Harper Collins College Publishers.

Vogel, Susan, ed. 1988. *The Art of Collecting African Art.* New York: The Center for African Art.

Vogel, Susan and Mary Nooter Roberts. 1994. *Exhibitionism: Museums and African Art.* New York: The Museum for African Art.

Wall Street Journal. 1992. "Rubber Tomahawks" (4 November):A14.

WalkingStick, Kay. 1992. "Native American Art in the Postmodern Era." *Art Journal* 51(3):15–17.

Washburn, Dorothy K. 1995. *Living in Balance: The Universe of the Hopi, Zuni, Navajo, and Apache.* Philadelphia: University of Pennsylvania Museum.

Wasserman, Abby. 1986. Portfolio. San Francisco: American Indian Contemporary Arts.

Way, J. Edson. 1993. "The Modern Gallery Exhibition as a Form of Western-Indigenous Discourse." Pp. 109–28 in *Imagery and Creativity,* edited by Dorothea and Norman Whitten. Tucson: University of Arizona Press.

Weigle, Marta. 1989. "From Desert to Disney World: The Santa Fe Railway and the Fred Harvey Company Display the Indian Southwest." *Journal of Anthropological Research* 45(1):115–37.

Weiner, Daniel H. 1995. "NAGPRA: Legal Burden or Historic Opportunity?" *Tribal Arts* 2(1):10–12.

Weisberg, Louis. 1989. "Activism, Art Unite Brothers." *Albuquerque Journal North* (15 August):29, 46.

White, Richard. 1997. "Representing Indians: Art, History, and the New Museums." *New Republic* 216(16):28–34.

White, Timothy. 1988. "Out of the Darkness: The Transformational Art of R. E. Bartow." *Shamans' Drum* (summer):16–23.

Whitehorse, Emmi. 1996. Conversation with author. Santa Fe, N.Mex., 27 June.

Whyte, Malcolm. 1995. "Collecting American Indian Art." In *Dancing Across Time: Indian Images of the Southwest.* San Francisco: American Indian Contemporary Arts.

Wolfe, John. 1996. "The Top 100: Collectors and Caretakers Share Their Treasures." *Art & Antiques* 19(3):8.

Wolfe, Tom. 1970. *Radical Chic and Mau-Mauing the Flak Catchers.* New York: Farrar, Straus and Giroux.

———. 1975. *The Painted Word.* New York: Bantam Books.

Wyatt, Victoria. 1984. *Shapes of Their Thoughts: Reflections of Culture Contact in Northwest Coast Indian Art.* Norman: University of Oklahoma Press.

Wye, Deborah. 1988. *Committed to Print: Social and Political Themes in Recent American Political Art.* New York: Museum of Modern Art.

Yazzie, Kelvin. 1994. Presentation at Atlatl conference, "The Artist as Community Healer." Portland, Oreg.

Yuxweluptun, Laurence Paul. 1995. "Artist's Statement." Pp. 1–6 in *Lawrence Paul Yuxweluptun: Born to Live and Die on Your Colonialist Reservations,* edited by Charlotte Townsend-Gault, Scott Watson, and Lawrence Paul Yuxweluptun. Vancouver: University of British Columbia.

Zimmer, William. 1995. "Light and Heat From American Indian Women." *New York Times* (24 September):20.

Abeyta, Tony, 66–67, 74, 80–81, 110

activism, 79–81, 106–7, 139–40. *See also* political art; politics and art

aesthetics: contemporary, 51; historical, 104–6; and the marketplace, 17; and politics, 141, 142; set by science, 20. *See also* quality

African art, 42–43, 127, 158, 161

Ahayu:da, 24. *See also* war gods, Zuni

airport art. *See* tourist art

Alaska Commercial Company, 16

Alaska Steamship Company, 18

Alcatraz Island, 106, 165

alterity, 117, 127. *See also* translation

American Indian Art, 51

American Indian Community House Gallery/ Museum, 7

American Indian Contemporary Arts, 52

American Indian Movement, 165

American Museum of Natural History, New York City, 96

anthropology: early, 16–17, 147–48; preservation, 16–17, 19, 154, 160–61; and private collectors, 19; tradition, 44; viewed by Native American scholars, 149–50; viewed by non-Native Americans, 150–51

Antique Tribal Art Dealers Association, 23, 157

Archaeological Resources Protection Act, 23

art groups: Antique Tribal Art Dealers Association, 23,

157; Friends of Indian Art (Santa Fe), 72, 95; Hopi Tribal Museum Project, 98; Indian Arts and Crafts Association, 30, 157; Native American Artists Association, 38; Native American Art Studies Association, 51

artifacts vs. art, 5–6, 19–20, 102, 108–9, 155

Arts and Crafts Movement, 18

art shows, 4

art world, 8, 153

assimilation, 21, 106, 136

Atlatl, 117

auction sales, 4

Australian Aboriginal art, 79

authenticity: determined by museums, 83; in fine-arts market, 41–47; and multiculturalism, 74; vs. quality, 117; of replicas, 154–55; and tradition, 103

Baer, Joshua, 59, 61

Bartow, Rick, *118*, 119

baskets: Chemehuevi, 51; Northwest Coast, 58; Pomo, 4; and technology, 47; Washo, 20–21, 51

Becker, Howard S., 8, 102

Benjamin, Walter, 41

Berkhofer, Robert, 12

Bhabha, Homi K., 131–33

Bigfeather, Joanna O.: ceramic sculptures, 159; on collecting, 141; her work, *14*, *144*; political art, 121, 140

bird feathers, 23
Birdie Brown auction, 51
Biss, Earl, 30
blankets, Navajo, *60*, 61
"blood", 156
Boas, Franz, 17
Boasian universalism, 19–20
Boyd, Alfred, *2*
Bradley, David, 32, 36, 38–39, 141
British Museum, 15
Brody, J. J., 6, 104–6

Canadian Native art, 156, 166
casinos, 28, 97
censorship, 163–64
Chemehuevi baskets, 51
Chippewas, 28
Christie's, 4, 41
Cicero, Jan, 130
citizenship, 21–22
Clifford, James, 10, 44, 84
Coe, Ralph T., 58
Coffin, Doug, *120*, 122
collecting: from battlefields, 22–23; as charity, 159–160; criticism of, 139–141; historical, 13, 15–16; private, 52–53; and the relationship with the artist, 9. *See also* anthropology; museums; tourism
collectors: community, 6, 8, 55–56; vs. decorators, 56–58; desire for exotic objects, 15, 73; desire for spirituality, 31, 42, 59; feeling of connection to the land, 63; first European, 15; interpretation of art, 142–45; and political art, 143–45; and "primitive" art, 159; relationships with artists, 127, 130, 131; vs. tourism, 59, 135–36
Collier, John, 29
colonialism, 147–48, 163
commodification, 40, 94–96, 155
community, 153
Corrow, Richard, 23–24, 160
counterfeits, 156–57. *See also* forgery; imitations
Creation's Journey (Smithsonian), 88
criticism, art, 110, 112, 114, 121, 122–23

Culin, Stewart, 17, 86–87
cultural patrimony, 23–24
culture-area model, 5

Dahl, Kathleen, 97
Danay, Richard Glazer, 140
Dat-so-la-lee, 51
David, Joe, 142
Day, Frank, 159–60
decorators vs. collectors, 56–58
Deloria, Vine, 32
discrimination, 21–22. *See also* ethnic identity, defined; stereotypes
displacement of material culture: first European, 11–12; modern view of, 22–23, 140–41; as preservation, 17, 19; repatriation, 23–26, 40, 83, 156
Dunn, Dorothy, 106
Durham, Jimmie, 39–40, 133

environmentalism, 80, 119, 142, 164
ethnic identity, defined, 28, 30, 32. *See also* Indian Arts and Crafts Act of 1990
ethnography, "new," 149
exhibits, 29, 88. *See also* museums
exotic objects, 15, 73, 110

Faulstich, Dale, 44
feathers, 23
Fenimore House Museum (Cooperstown), 53
filmmaking, 159
fine art, 5, 36, 41, 108–9, 164
Fine, Joan and Steve, *60*
folk art, 5
Fonesca, Harry, 115, *116*
forgery, 41–43, 157–58. *See also* counterfeits
Fred Jones Jr. Museum of Art (University of Oklahoma), 52
Freund, Thatcher, 56
Friends of Indian Art (Santa Fe), 72, 95
funerary objects, 23

galleries, 5, 44
gaming, 28, 97, 142
General Allotment Act, 21, 28–29
Giago, Tim, 98
gift shops, 95
Gill, Sam, 13, 154
glass, 74, *75*, *76*, 77
Gordon, Beverly, 16
Goshorn, Shan, 121
Gottlieb, Adolph, 20, 115
Graburn, Nelson, 85–86
Greenberg, Clement, 109–10

Haas, Jim, 20–21
Haozous, Bob, 117, 119, 121
Harjo, Suzan, 32
d'Harnoncourt, Rene, 29, 103
Heap of Birds, Edgar Hachivi, 134, 140
Heye, George Gustav, 8, 22, 87, 163
Holm, Bill, 44
Hopis, 43
Hopi Tribal Museum Project, 98
Houser, Alan, 73, 167–68
Hoving, Thomas, 41

"imagined" Indian, 11–13, 30, 104, 142
imitations, 30. *See also* counterfeits; forgery
Indian Artist, 160
Indian Art of the United States (Museum of Modern Art), 29
Indian Arts and Crafts Act of 1990, 31–40, 78–79
Indian Arts and Crafts Association, 30, 157
Indian Arts and Crafts Board, 31, 103, 156
Indian Arts and Crafts Board Act of 1935, 27, 28–30
Indian Market (Santa Fe), 137, 139, 155
Indian Painters and White Patrons (Brody), 104–6
"Indian time," 128–30. *See also* stereotypes
Institute of American Indian Arts (Santa Fe), 30, 71–73, 107, 139–40, 162
internet trading posts, 59
Ishi and the Wood Ducks (Vizenor), 36, 38

Jacknis, Ira, 44
Jojola, Tony, 77, 159

kachinas, 43
Kroeber, Alfred, 38

LaMarr, Jean, 107
Lavadour, James, 162
Left Handed Kachina (Shepard), 125–26
legislation: Archaeological Resources Protection Act, 23; citizenship, 21–22; General Allotment Act, 21, 28–29; on identity of tribes, 28, 30, 32; Indian Arts and Crafts Board Act of 1935, 27, 28–30; Migratory Game Bird Act, 23; Omnibus Trade Bill, 30, 31; repatriation, 23–26; *Santa Clara Pueblo v. Martinez* (U.S. Supreme Court), 157. *See also* Indian Arts and Crafts Act of 1990
Lelooska, 158–59
Lemann, Nicholas, 42
LePena, Frank, 115, 117
Lévi-Strauss, Claude, 85
LewAllen Cline Gallery, 5
Lewis and Clark, 16
Little Turtle, Carm, 39
Lobb, Alan, 58
Lomahaftewa, Dan V., 67–68, *69*, 70, 77, 78
Louisiana Purchase, 16
Luna, James, *132*, 133

MacCannell, Dean, 9
Manoogian, Richard, 58
marketplace, 4–5, 17–19, 110. *See also* collecting
Masayesva, Victor, 159
masks, 16, 20, 23–24, 60
Mason, Otis T., 155
material culture. *See* collecting; displacement of material culture
McCabe, Michael, 5
Migratory Game Bird Act, 23
Mitchell, Nancy. *See* Mithlo, Nancy
Mithlo, Nancy, 73, 121

modernism vs. primitivism, 73–74, 107–8, 115, 117, 157. *See also* stereotypes
Morgan, Lewis Henry, 12, 154
"Mother Earth," 154
multiculturalism, 74, 114, 123, 145
museology, new, 84
Museum of Modern Art, New York City, 29
Museum of the American Indian (Smithsonian), 92, *93*
museums: American Museum of Natural History, 96; Canadian, 52; and censorship, 163–64; and dissidence, 87–88, 96; Fenimore House Museum (Cooperstown), 53; first European collections, 15; Fred Jones Jr. Museum of Art (University of Oklahoma), 52; Friends of Indian Art (Santa Fe), 72, 95; Museum of Modern Art, 29; National Museum of the American Indian (Smithsonian), 8, 23, 84, 89–94, 156; Northwest Coast collection (British Museum), 15; Peabody Museum of Archaeology and Ethnology (Harvard University), 16; Portland Art Museum, 88; and repatriation, 86; Southwest Museum (Los Angeles), 95; and their visitors, 85–86, 92, 163; tribal, 97
Myers, Fred, 6

Nailor, Gerald, *138*
Naranjo-Morse, Nora, *46*
National Museum of the American Indian (Smithsonian), 8, 23, 84, 89–94, 156
Native American Artists Association, 38
Native American Art Studies Association, 51
Native American Graves Protection and Repatriation Act, 23–25
Native Americans: citizenship, 21–22; ethnic identity, defined by law, 28, 30, 32; the "imagined" Indian, 11–13, 30; individualism, 65–66, 74; museum involvement, 88–89; populations, 16–17; tribal identity, 97. *See also* Indian Arts and Crafts Act of 1990
nature. *See* "imagined" Indian; environmentalism
Navajo: blankets, *60*, 61; jewelry, 53–55; masks, 23–24; weaving, 17, 59, 70, 155

New Deal, 28–29
NMAI. *See* National Museum of the American Indian (Smithsonian)
Norick, Frank, 43
Northwest Coast baskets, 58
Northwest Coast collection (British Museum), 15
Northwest Native Expressions, 44

Oglala Sioux, 25–26
Omnibus Trade Bill, 30, 31
Oxendine, Lloyd, 107

Pacheco, Andrew, 62
painting, easel, 104–6, 159
parfleche, 61
Parke Bernet. *See* Sotheby's
Pasco, Duane, 13, 44
Paul, Lawrence, 80. *See also* Yuxweluptun
Peabody Museum of Archaeology and Ethnology (Harvard University), 16
Pearce, Roy Harvey, 12
Peltier, Leonard, 78
Phillips, Ruth, 44–45
political art, 142–45. *See also* activism
politics and art: contemporary, 79–81, 139–41; criticism, 121–22; discrimination, 21; protests, 106–7; tribal input and museums, 88
Pomo baskets, 4
Portland Art Museum, 88
postmodernism, 134–35
potlatch materials, 155, 156
pottery, 47
preservation, 16–17, 19, 154, 160–161
primitivism vs. modernism, 73–74, 107–8, 115, 117, 157
primitivist discourse, 17, 20, 40–41
Pueblo Indians, 21–22

quality, 114–15, 117, 123. *See also* authenticity

Rabinowitz, Bev, 62
Reichard, Gladys, 17
repatriation, 23–26, 40, 83, 156
replicas, 154–55
Romero, Diego, 142
Roosevelt, Franklin D., 28, 29
Rushing, W. Jackson, 122–23
Russian American Company, 16

Sackler, Elizabeth, 156
Saginaw Chippewa tribe, 28
Sakiestewa, Ramona, 71
Santa Clara Pueblo v. Martinez (U.S. Supreme Court), 157
Santa Domingo Pueblo, 167
Santa Fe (N.Mex.), 5, 59, 137, 139, 155
Scholder, Fritz, 30
Schoolcraft, Henry Rowe, 13
Scottsdale (Ariz.), 5, 59
Seattle (Wash.), 5, 59
Shepard, Sam, 125–26
silver polishing, 161
silversmithing, 165
silverwork, 47
Singletary, Preston, 71, 74, *75*, *76*, 77
Sioux, Oglala, 25–26
S'Klallam tribe (Jamestown), 44
Smith, Jaune Quick-to-See, 142, 150
social evolution, 147–48
Sotheby's, 4, 51
Southwest Museum (Los Angeles), 95
Soza, Bill, 107, 165–66
spiritual power, 42, 59, 61. *See also* stereotypes
Steiner, Christopher, 6
stereotypes: in the media, 13, 127–28; of non-Indians, 167; and tourism, 137; used in political art, 142. *See also* "imagined" Indian; "Indian time"
Stone, Jason, 36
Strickland, Rennard, 52
Submuloc Show (Atlatl), 117, 119
surrealists, 20

Taos Pueblo (N.Mex.), 136–37
Thaw, Eugene, 53
Tlingits, 88
Torgovnick, Marianna, 40
tourism: vs. collectors, 59, 135–36; economics of, 136; effects on aesthetics, 18; "Indian Detours", 167; marketing of stereotypes, 13, 128
tourist art, 5, 40, 43, 44–45
trading posts, 153
tradition: and authenticity, 103; and collecting, 159; and other media, 164; and primitivism, 44–47; and quality, 108–9, 117
translation, 132–33
tribal identity, 28, 78, 97
Tsinhnahjinnie, Hulleah, *33–35*
Twitchell, Adams, 16
Two Bulls, Nellie, 26

Vancouver (B.C.), 59
Vancouver, George, 15
Vizenor, Gerald, 36, 38
Vogel, Susan, 42

WalkingStick, Kay, 22, *37*, 112, *113*, 162
Walt Disney World, 13
Walters, Roy "Dune," *2*
war gods, 24–25, 156. *See also* Ahayu:da, Zuni
Washo baskets, 20–21, 51
weaving, 17, 59, 70, 155. *See also* blankets, Navajo
West, Richard, 90
Whitehorse, Emmi, 81, 110, *111*, 112
White, Loren, 44
White, Randy Lee, 39
Whitney Museum of American Art, New York City, 131–33
Whyte, Karen, 52
Whyte, Malcolm, 52
Wilderness Lodge, 13
Wilson, Lyle, 108
Wolfe, Thomas, 49–50

Wounded Knee, 106–7, 165
Wounded Knee Survivors Association, 25

Yazz, Beatien, 139
Yazzie, Kelvin, 74
Yei B'Chei masks, 23–24

Youngblood, Nathan, 108
Yup'ik masks, 16, 20, 60
Yuxweluptun, 80, 134. *See also* Lawrence Paul

Zuni Pueblo, 167
Zunis, 24–25, 137, 156. *See also* Ahayu:da, war gods

3 3710 00089286 4